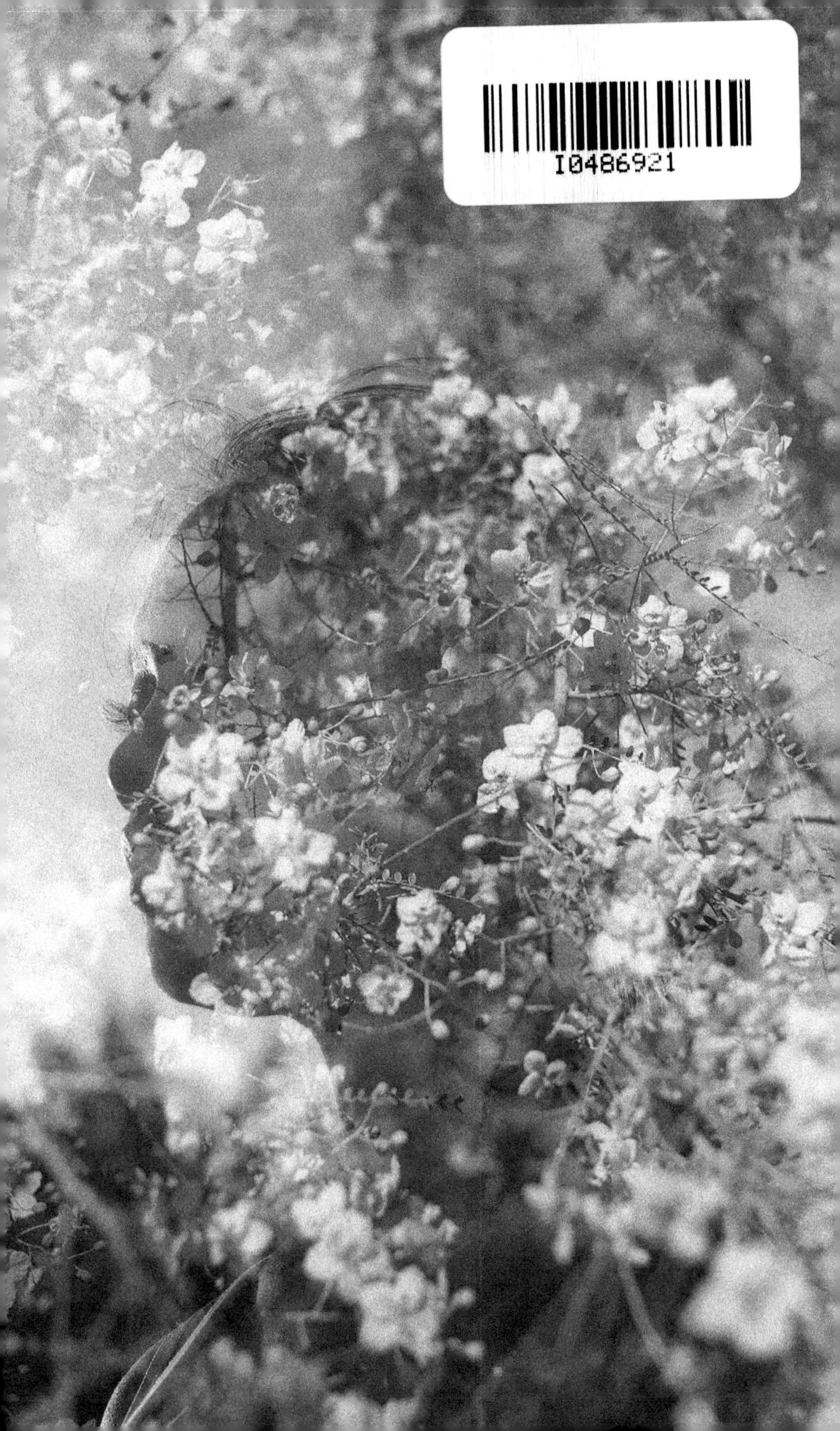

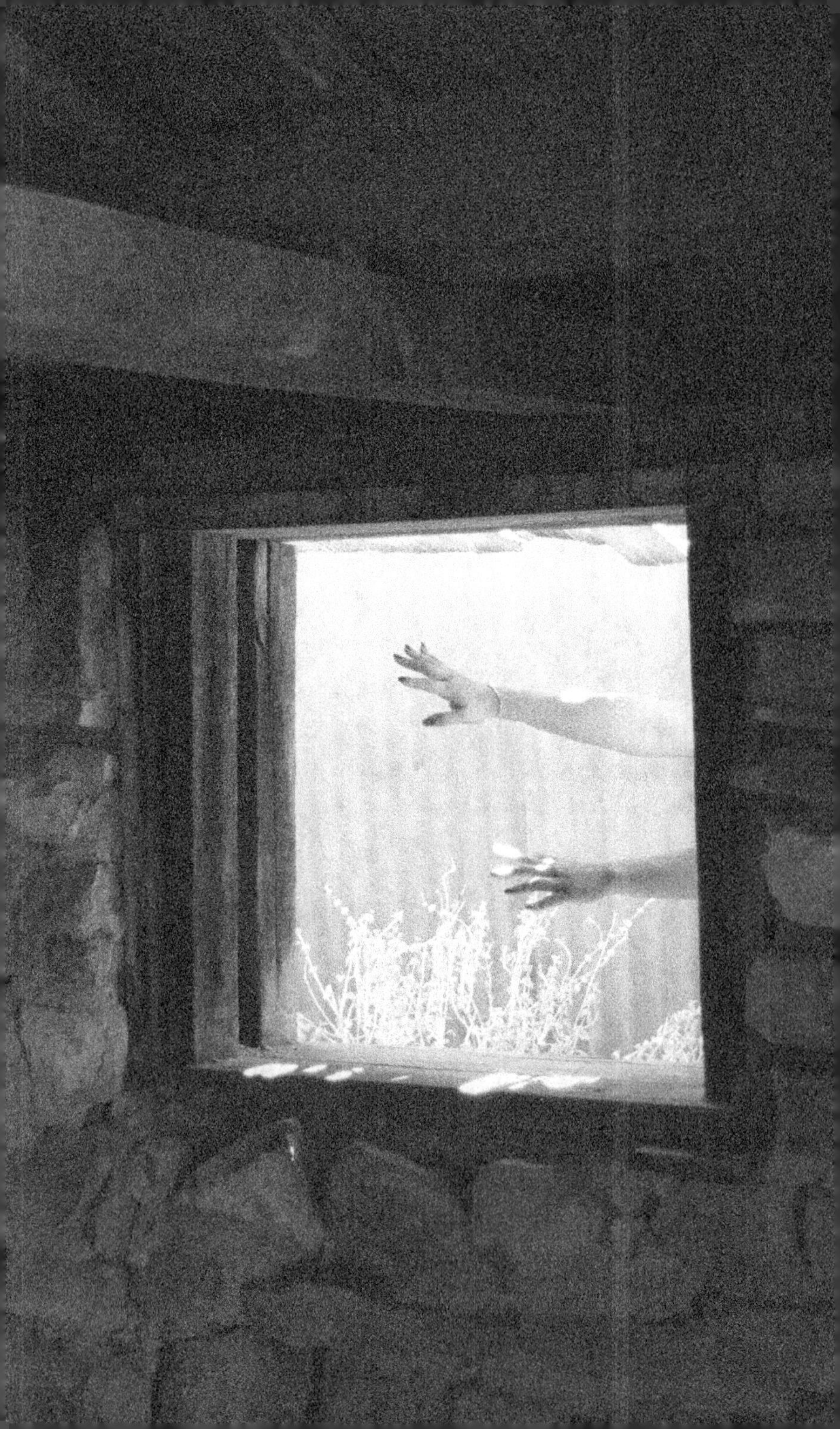

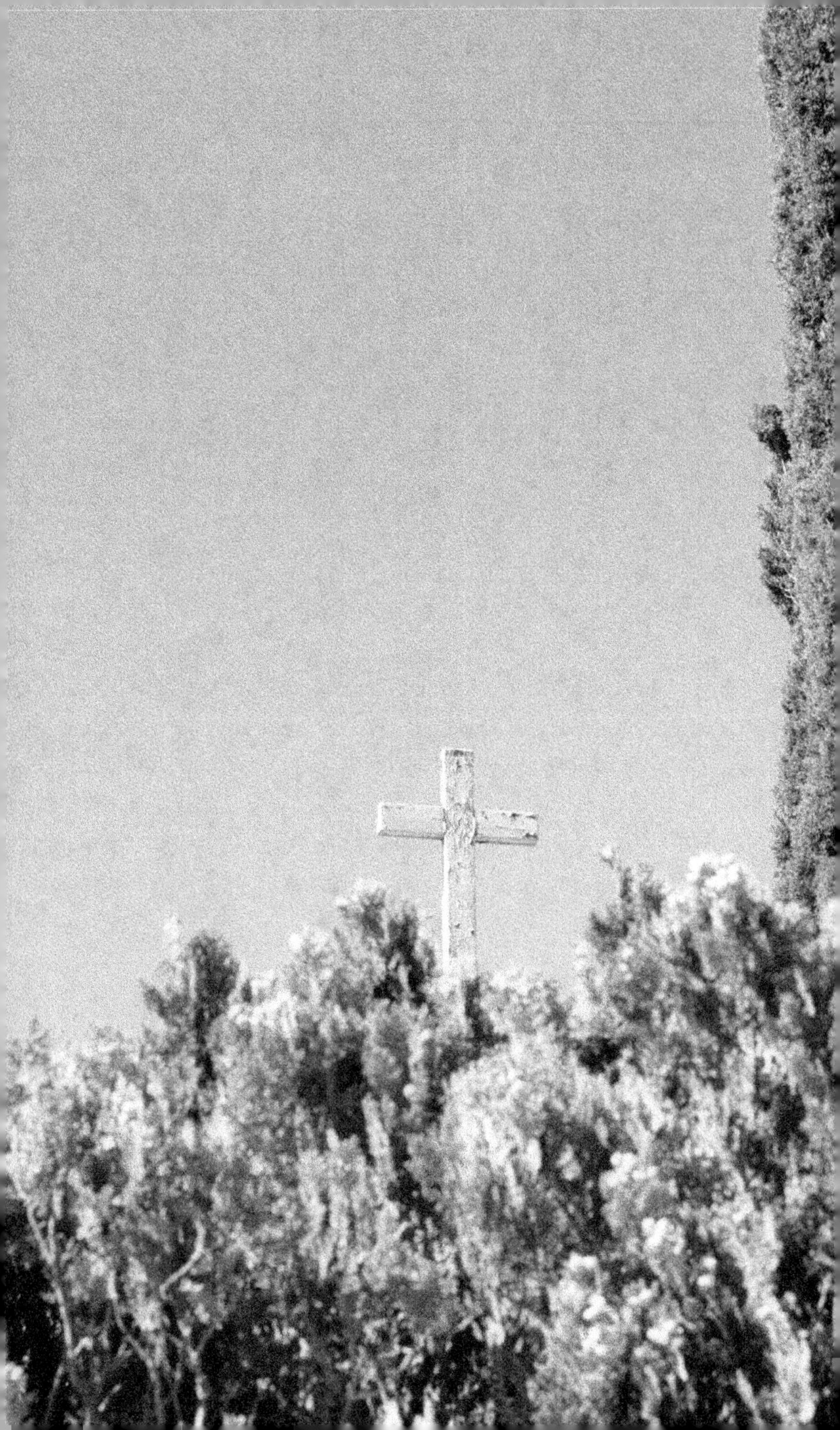

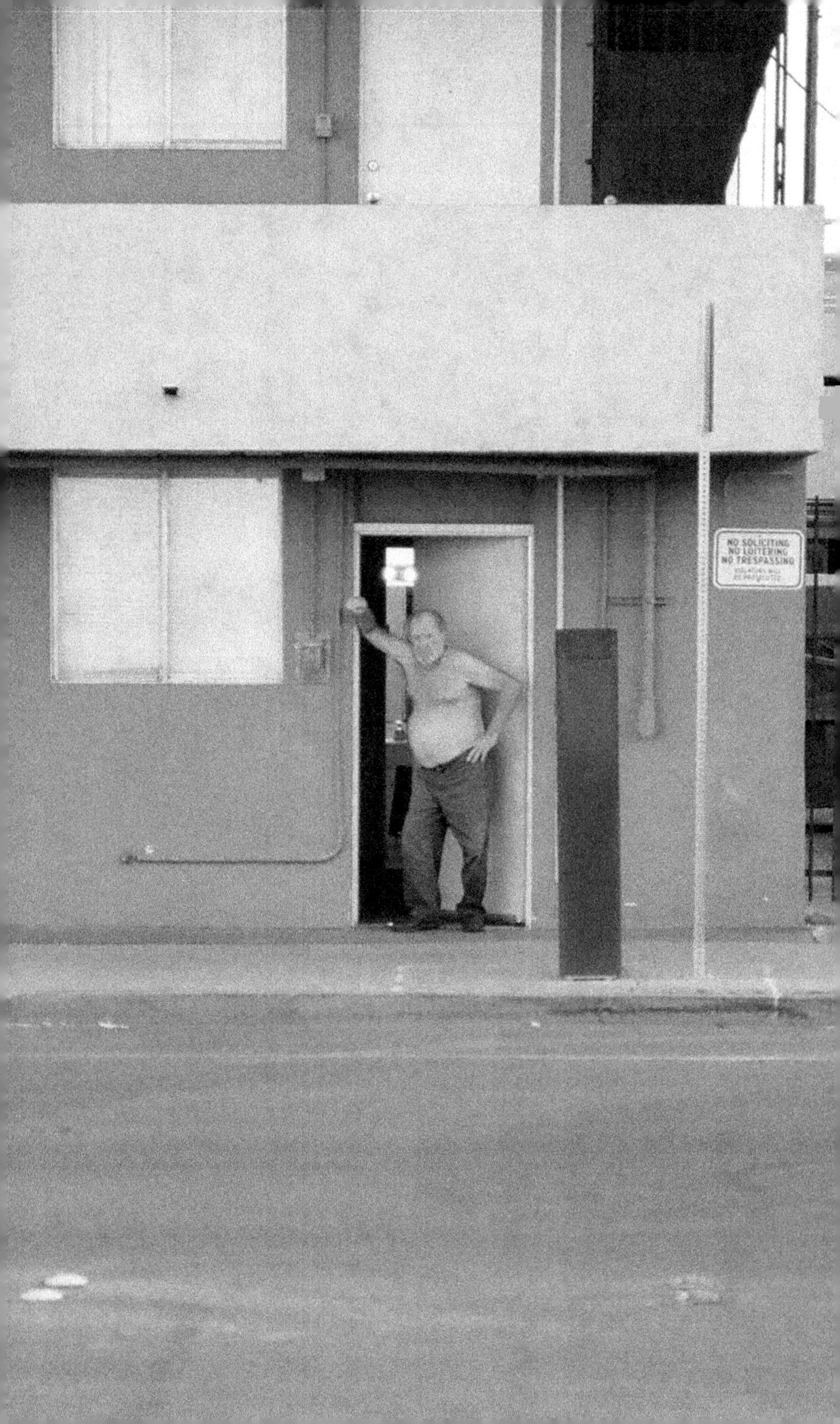
NO SOLICITING
NO LOITERING
NO TRESPASSING

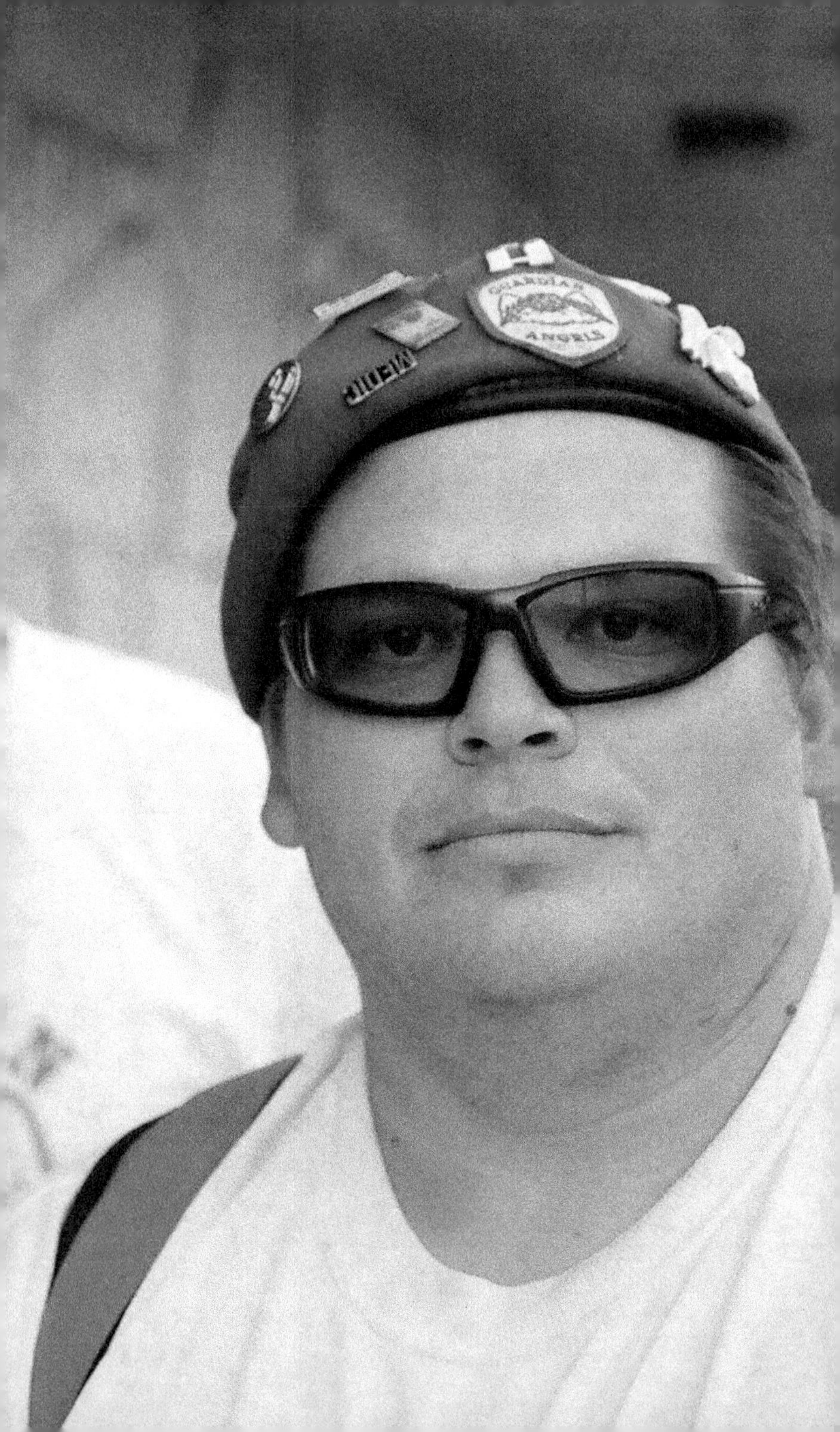
ANGELS

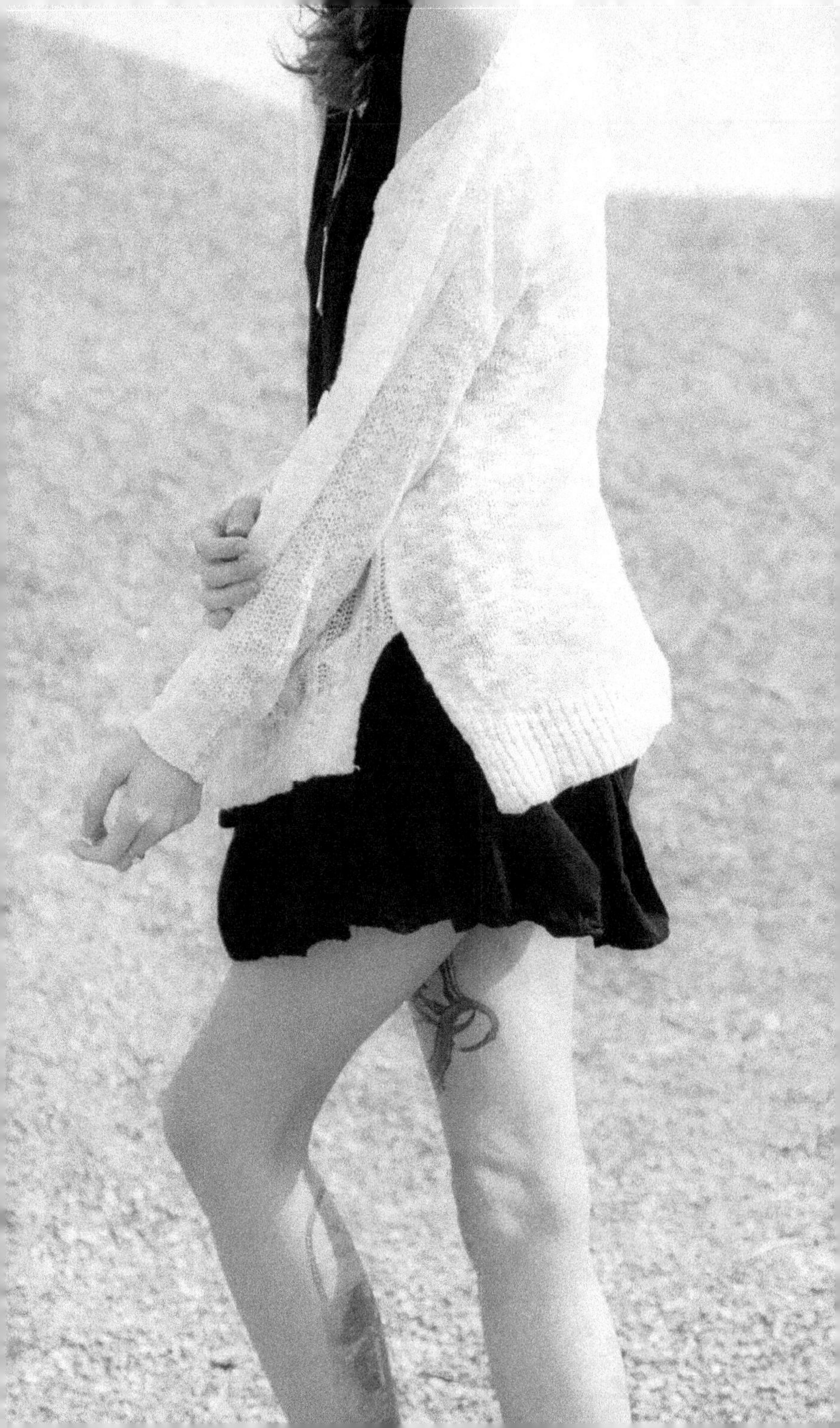

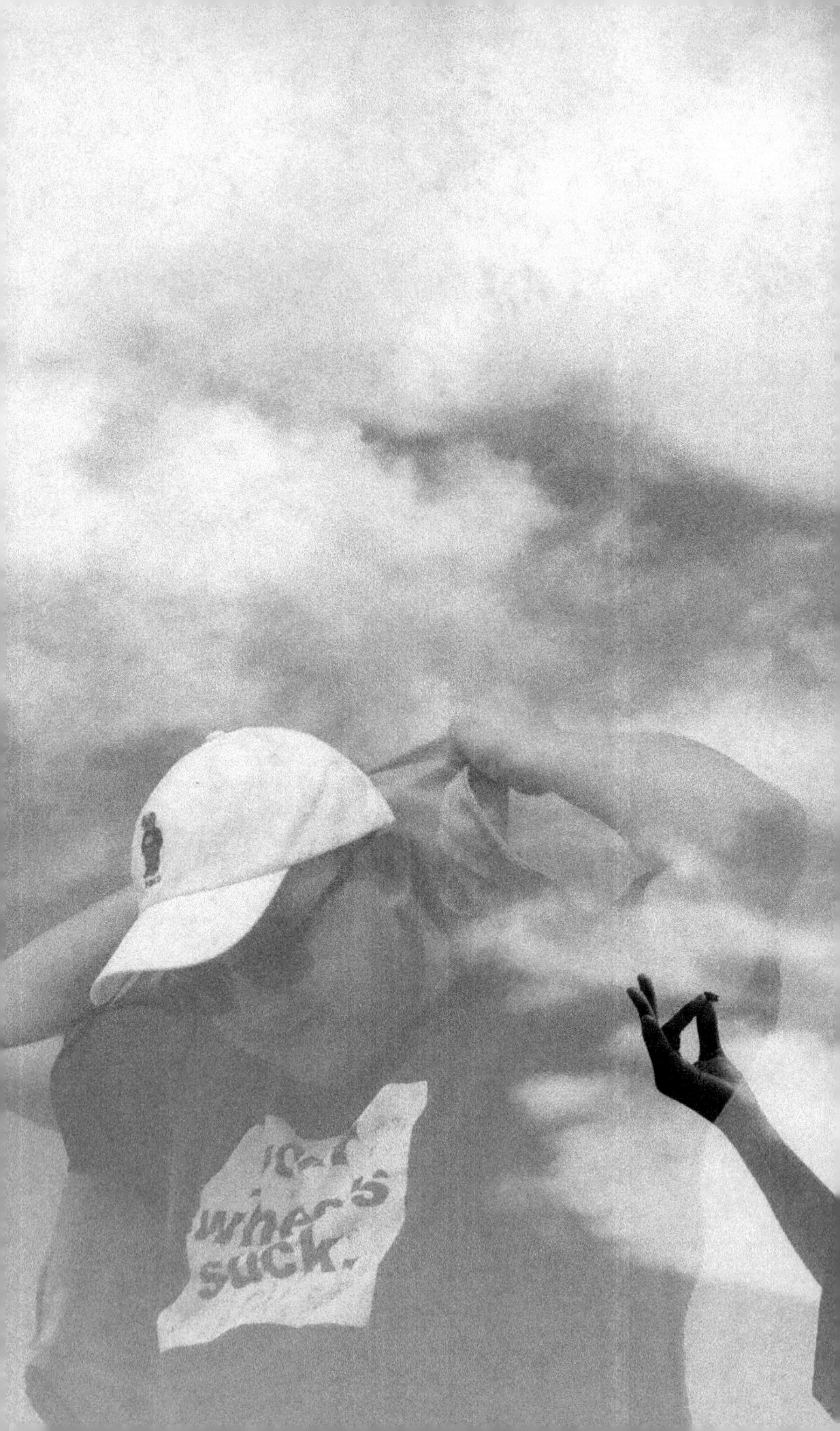
suck.

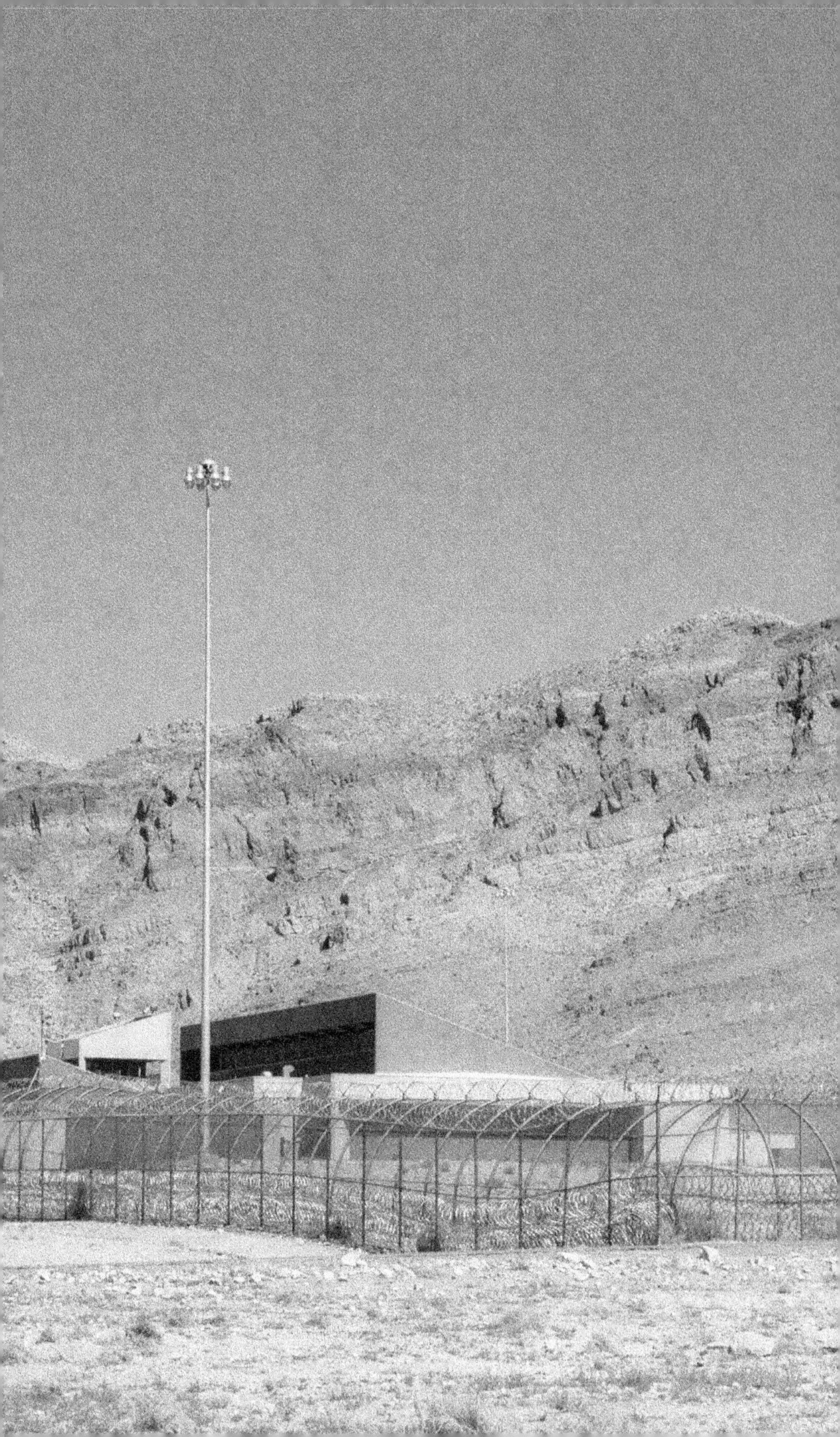

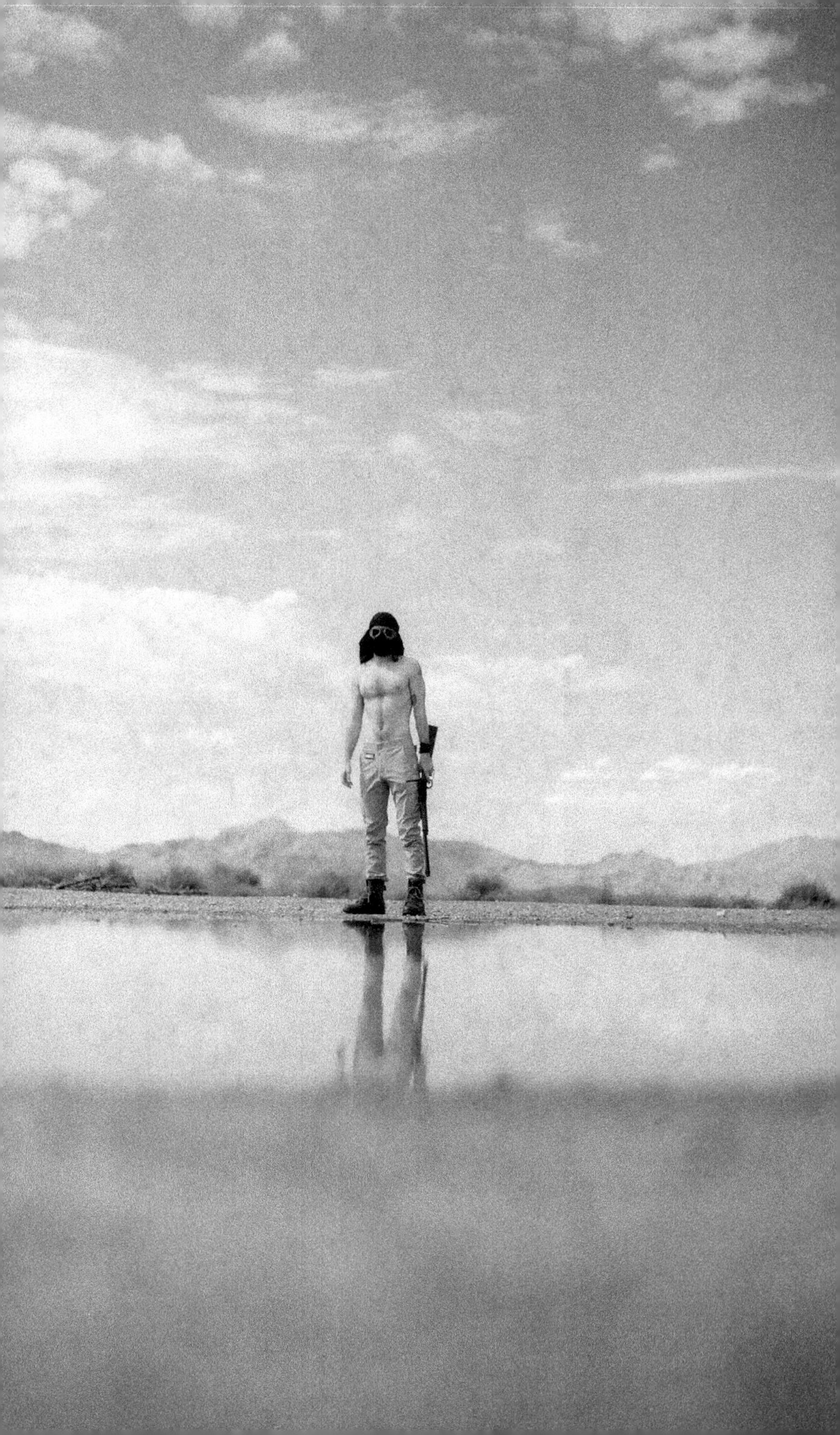

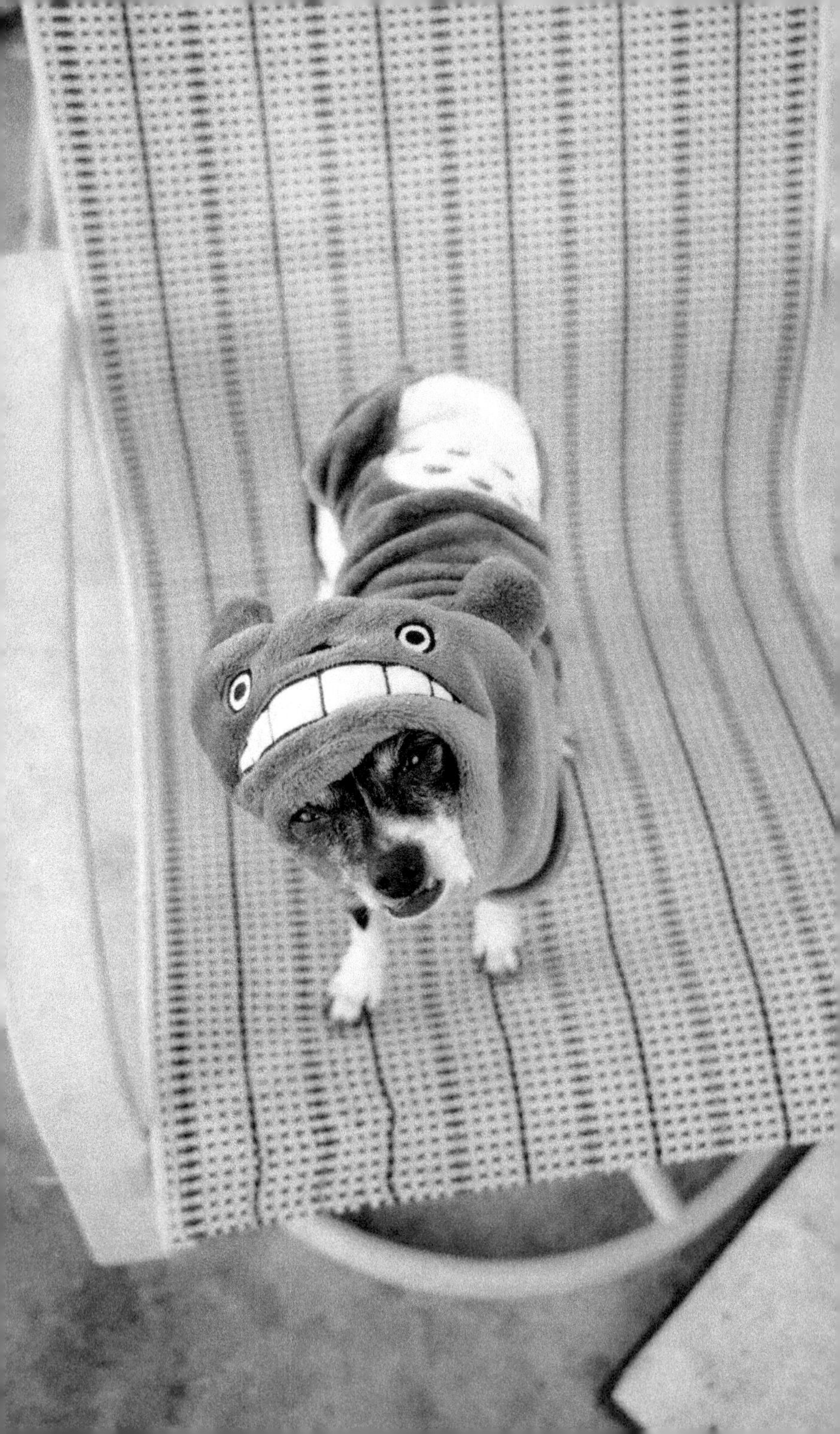

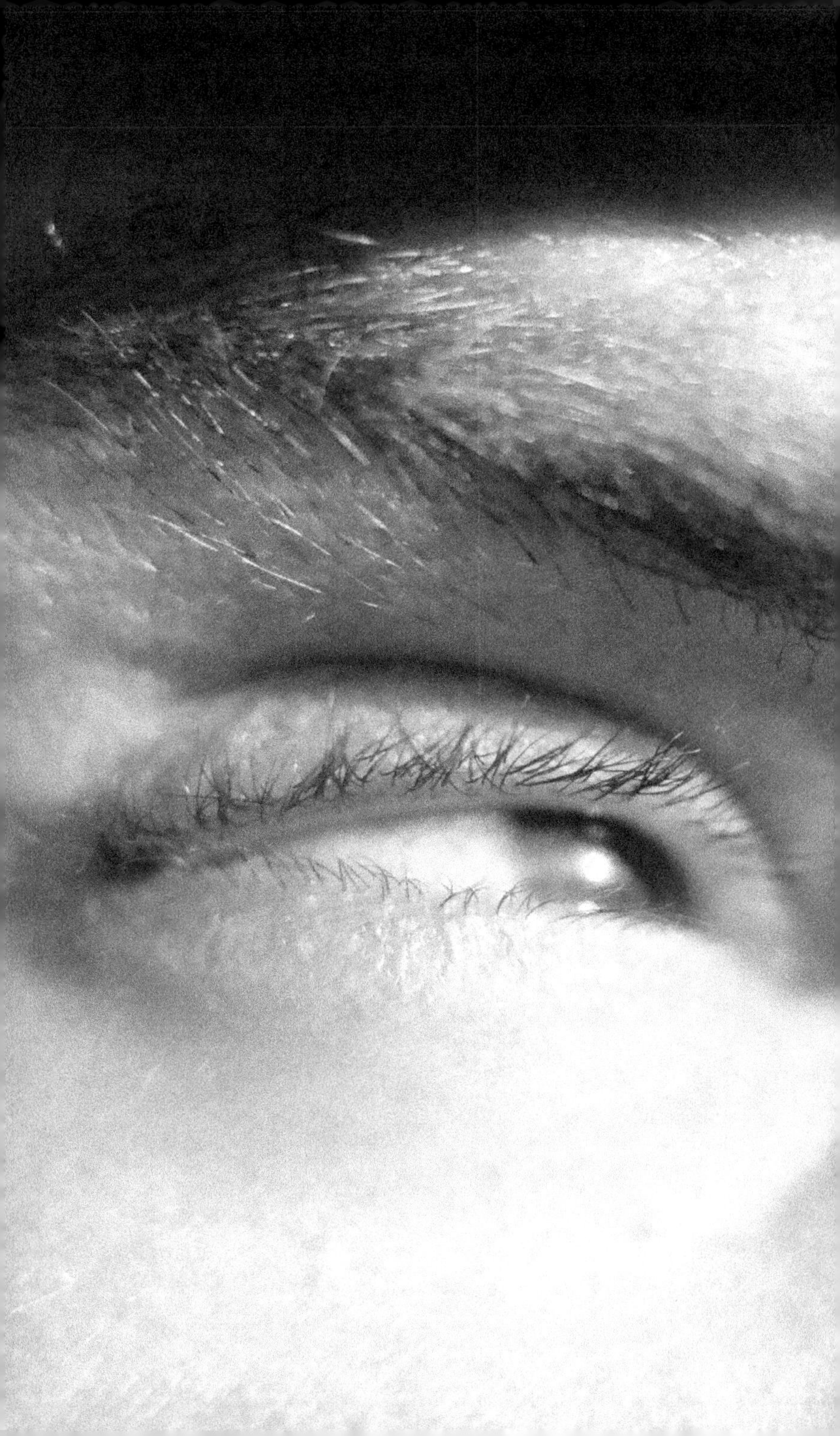

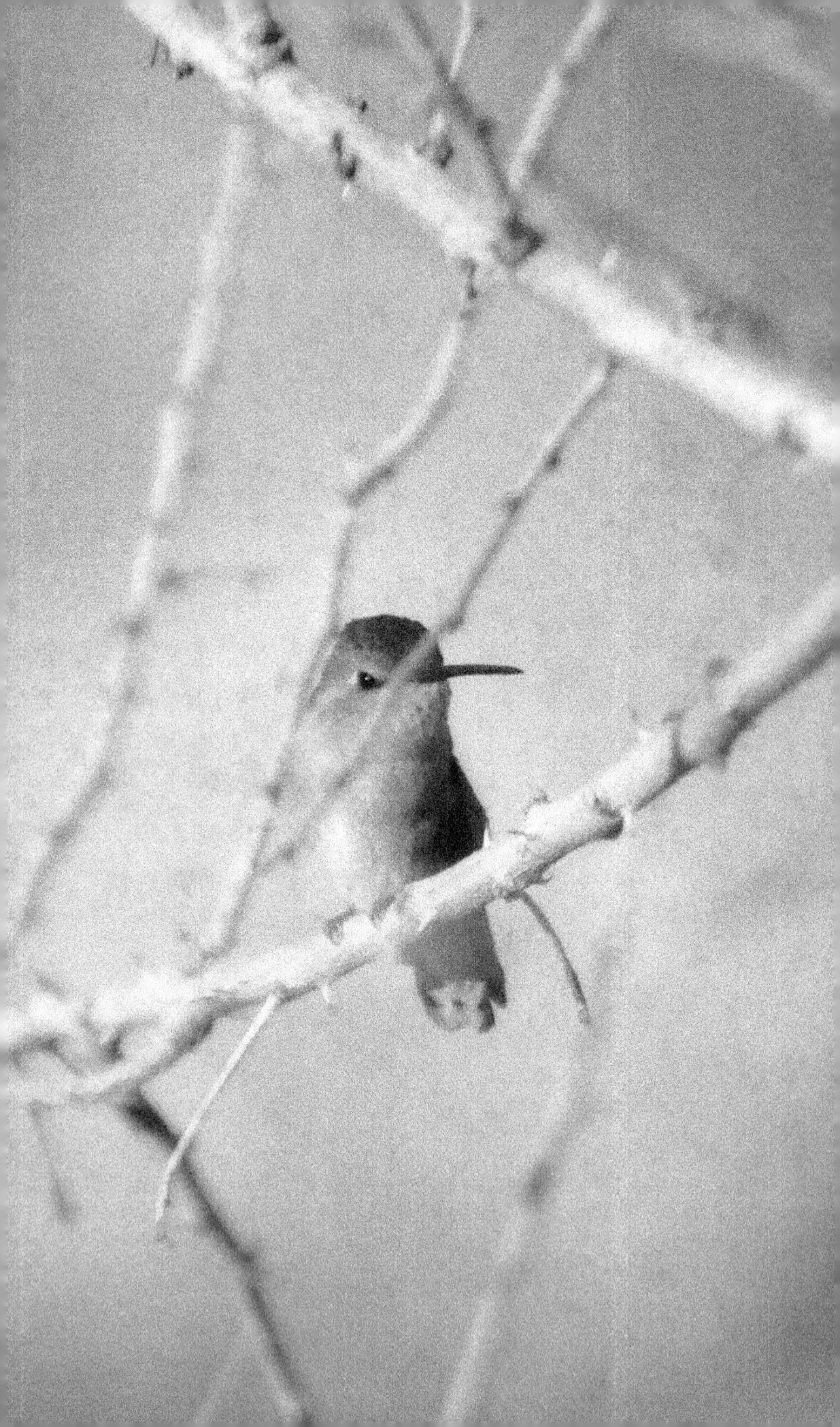

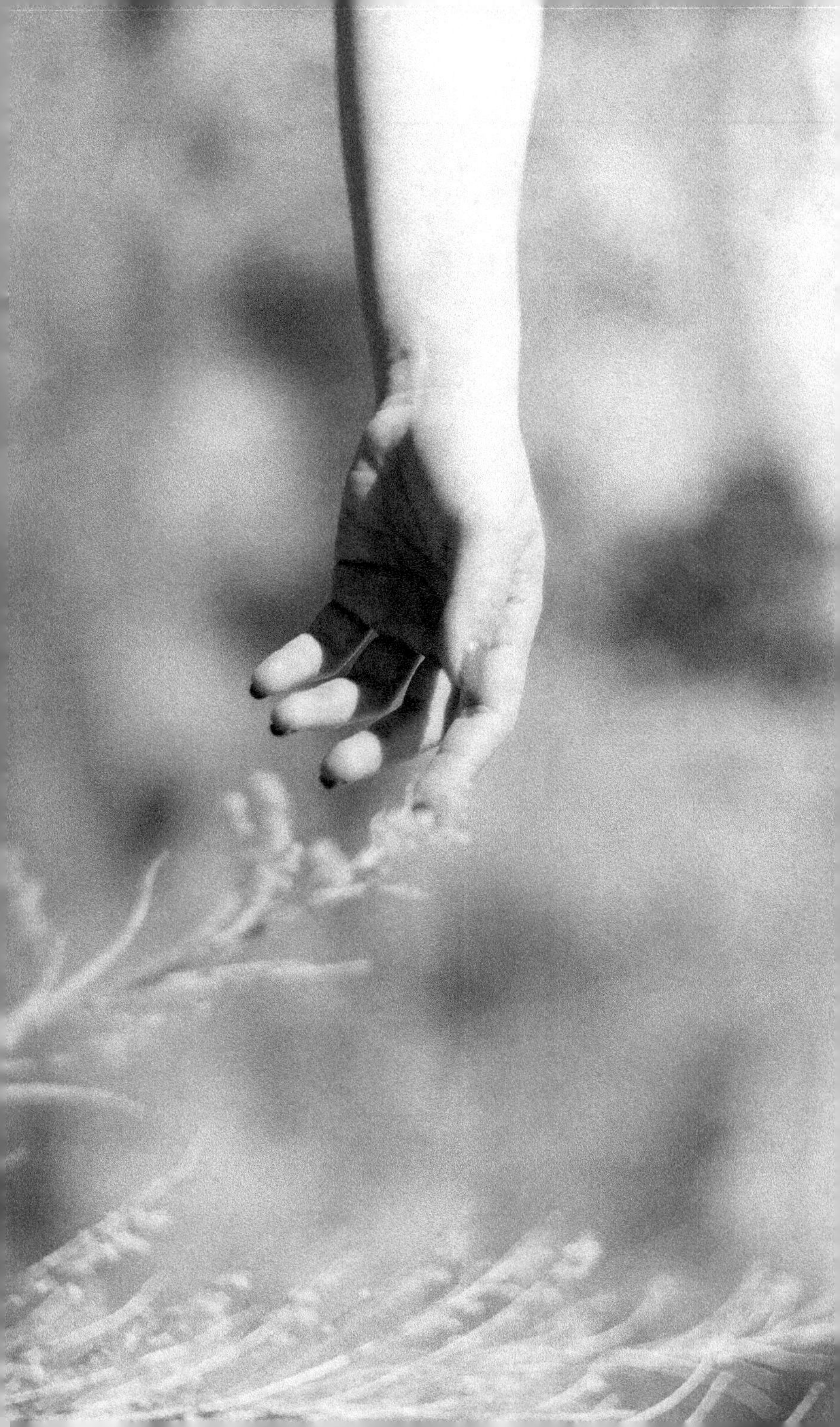

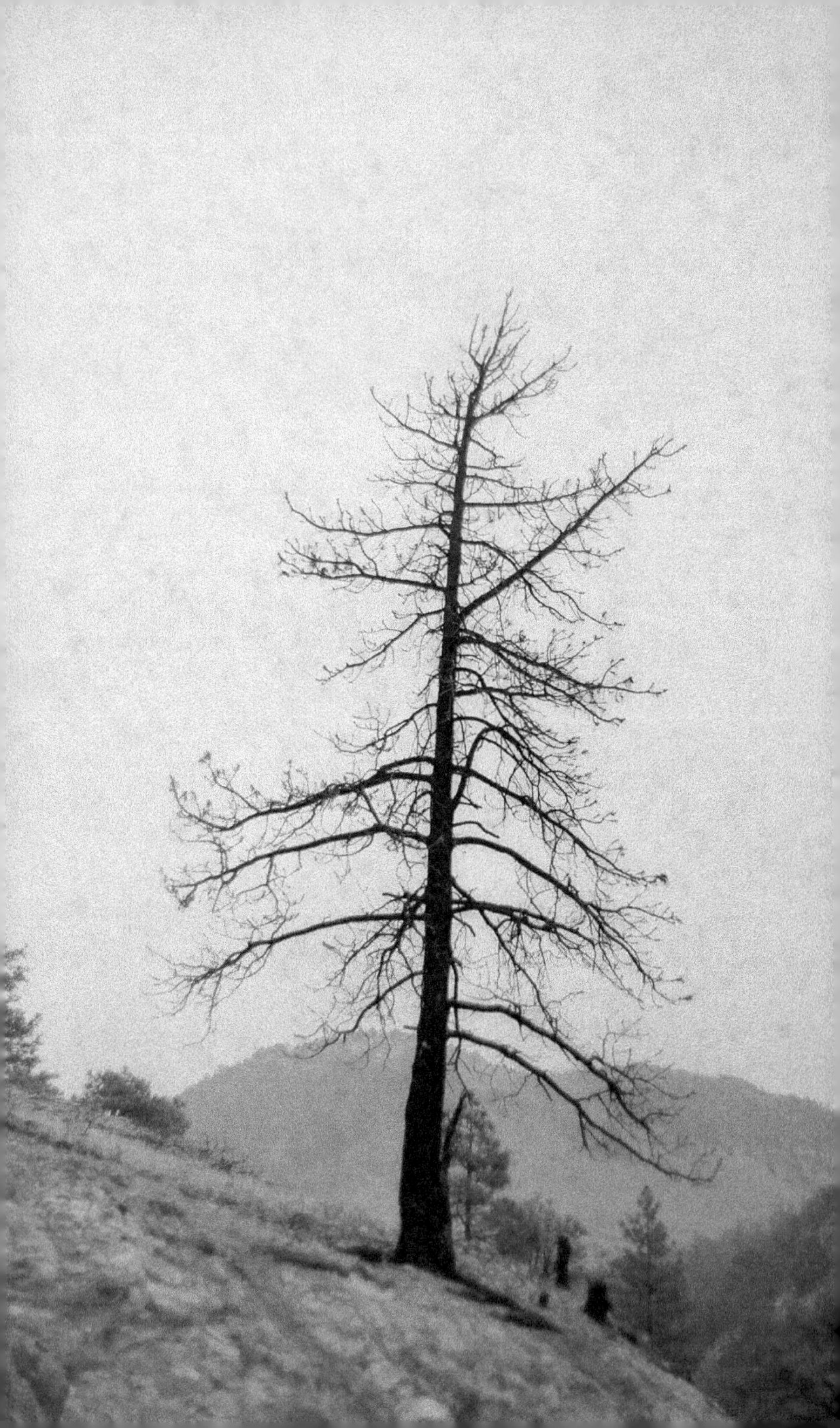

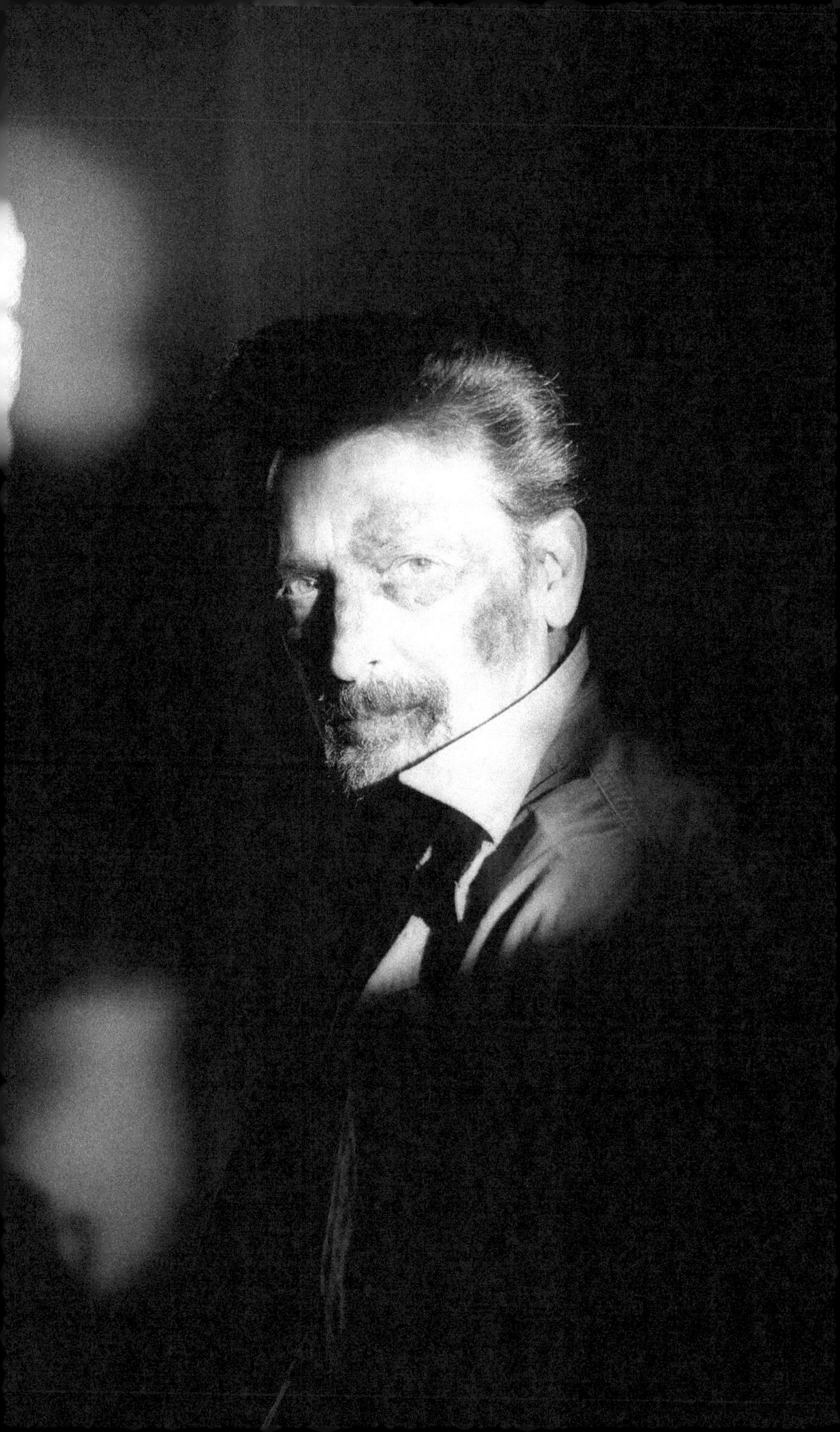

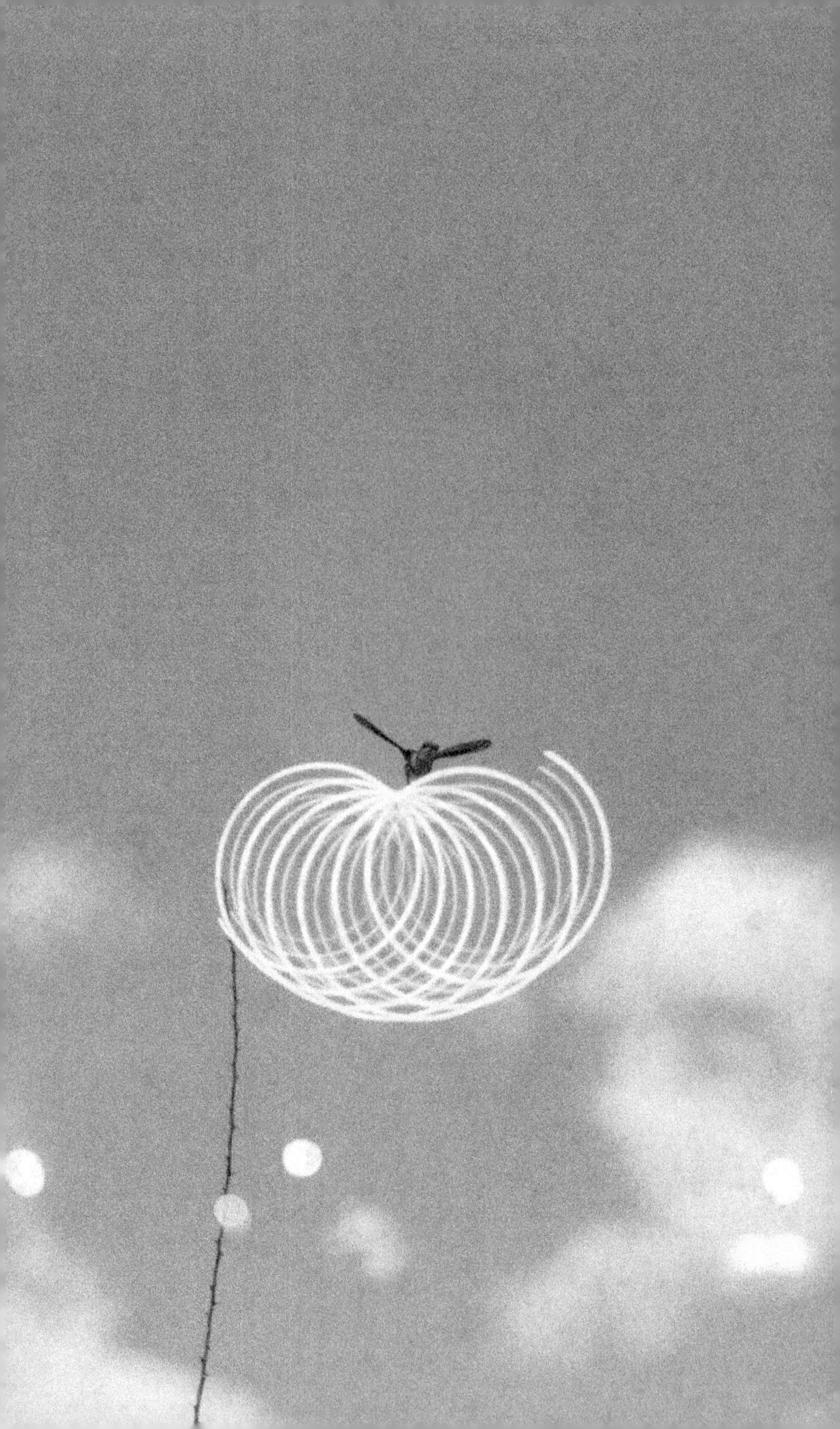

MIKE MOREY'S

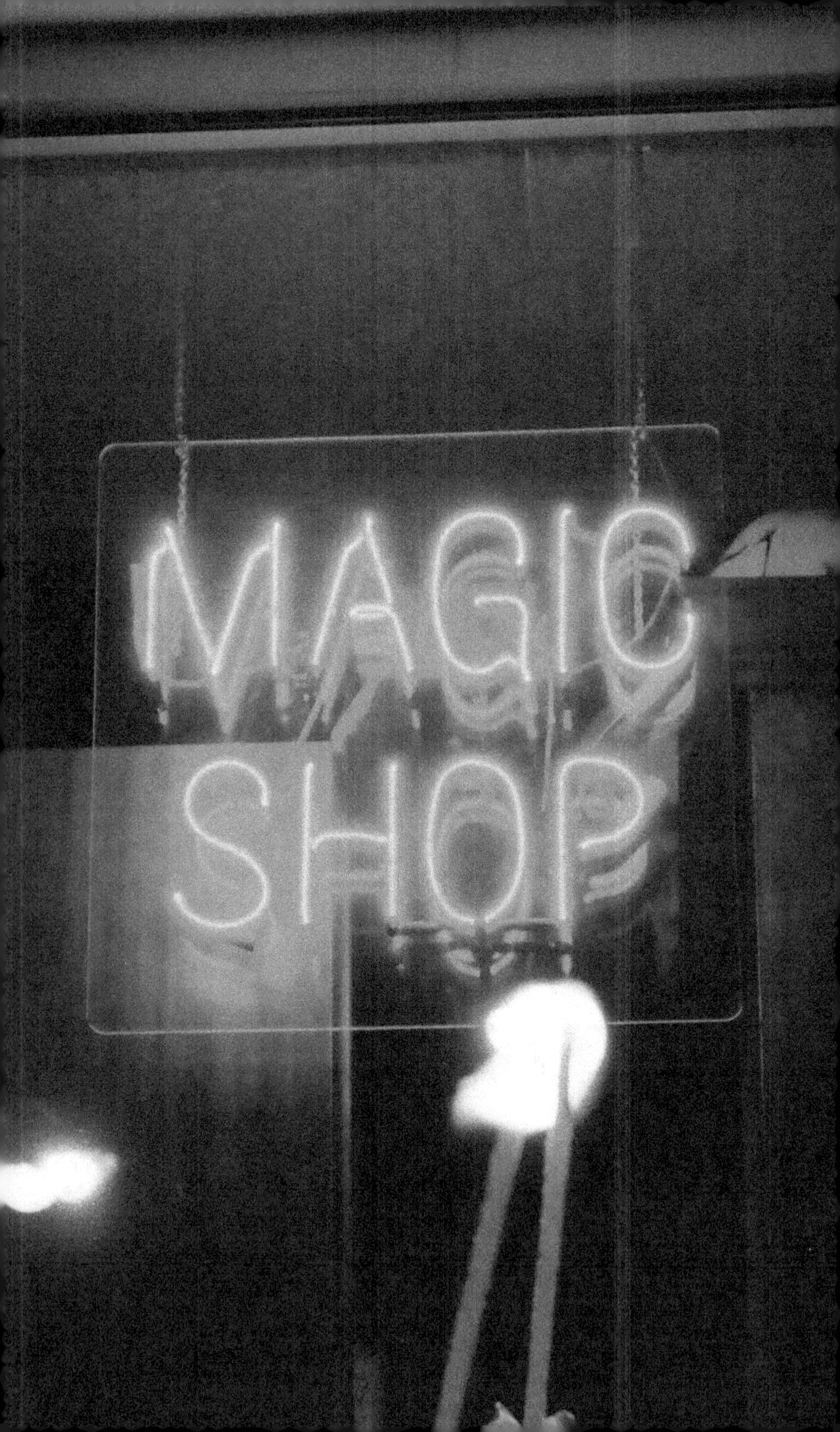
MAGIC
SHOP

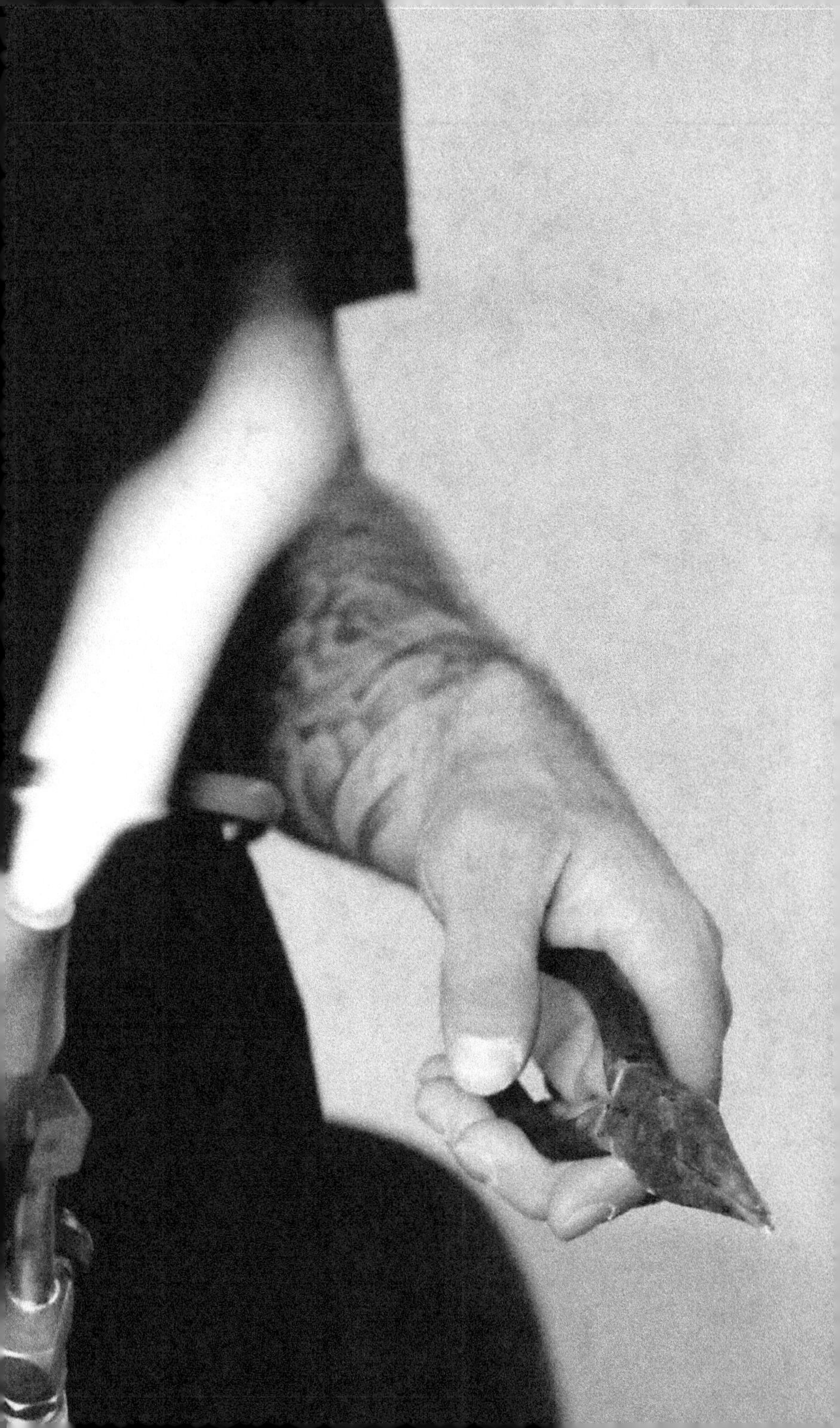

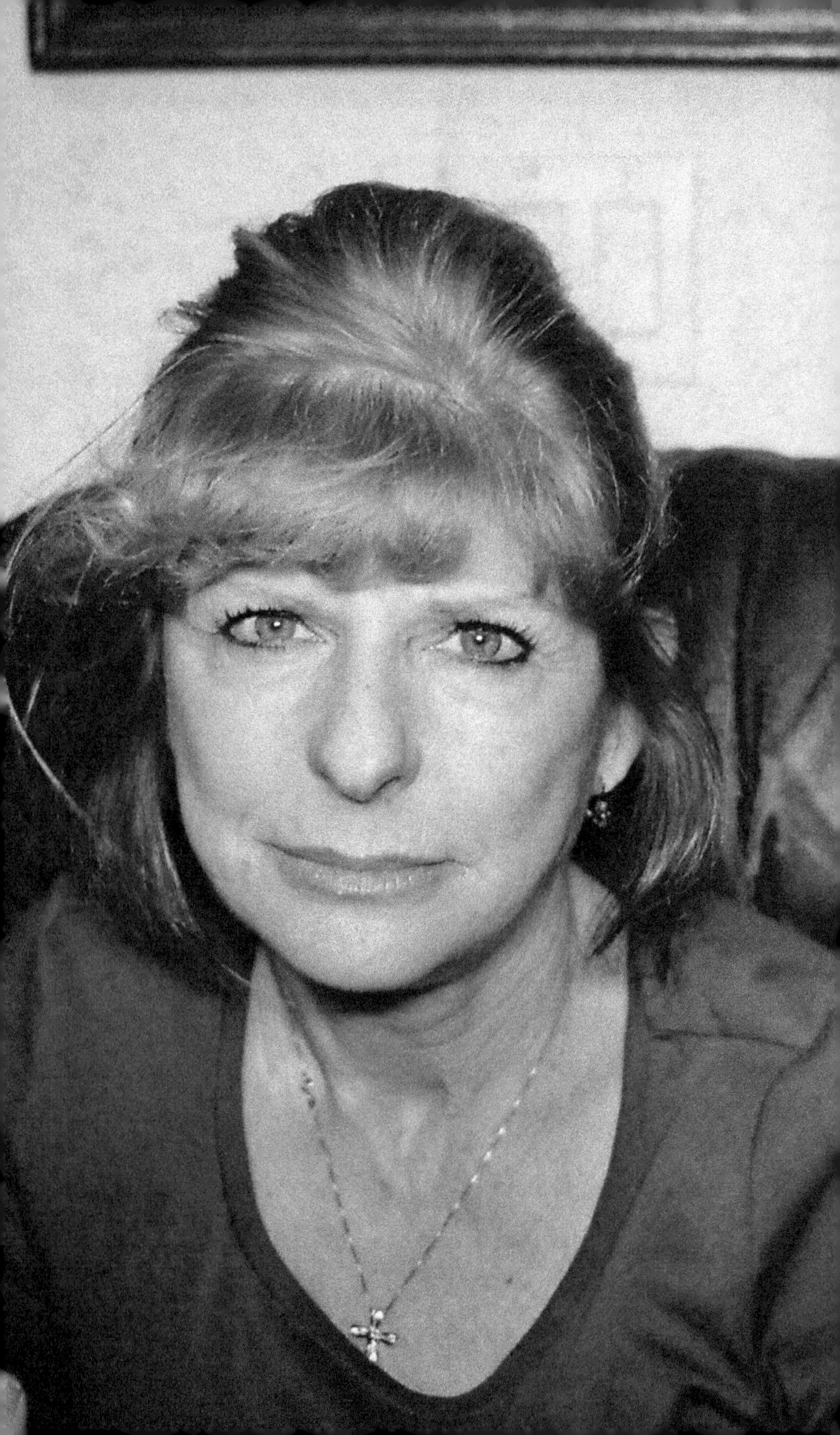

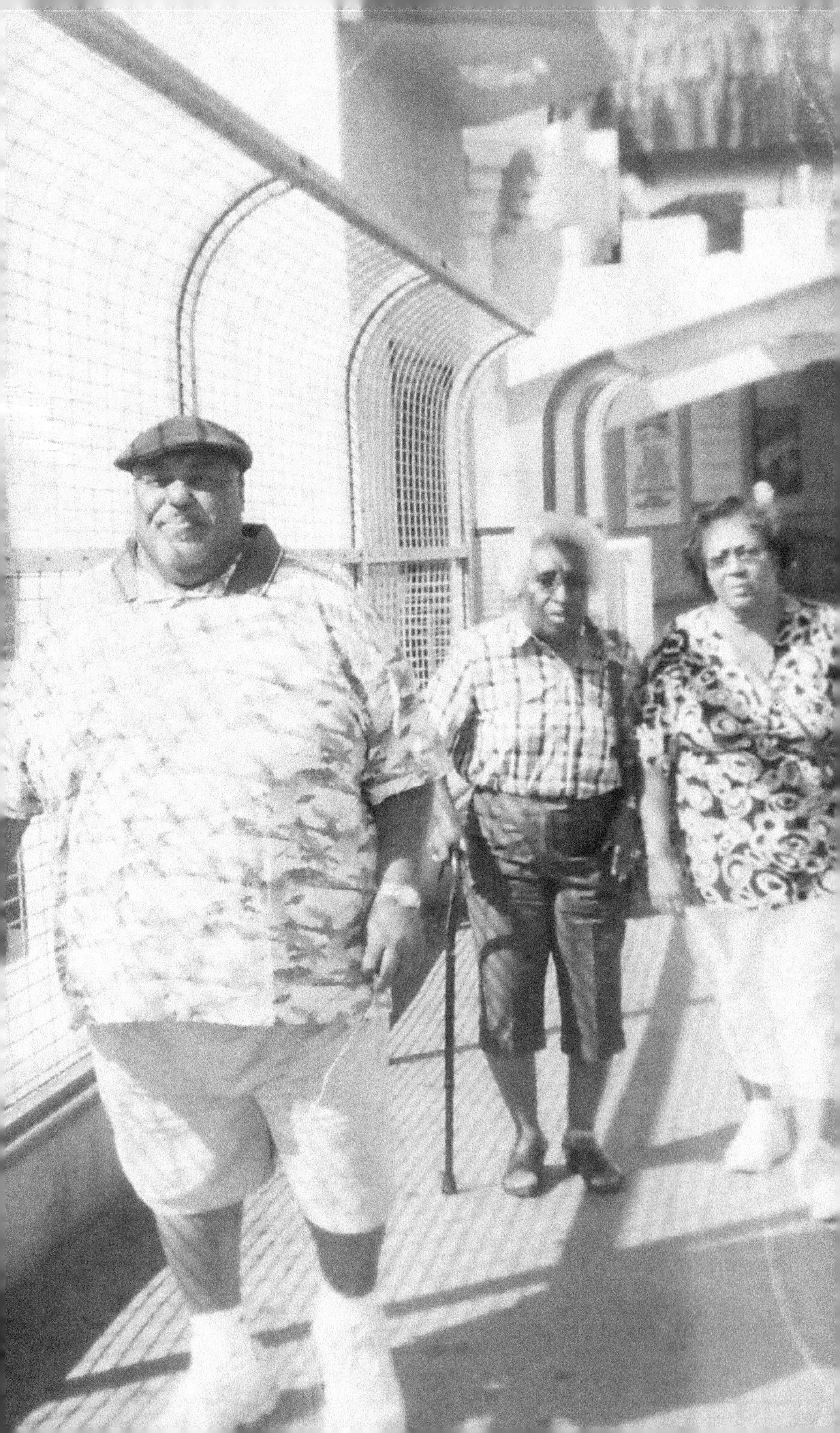

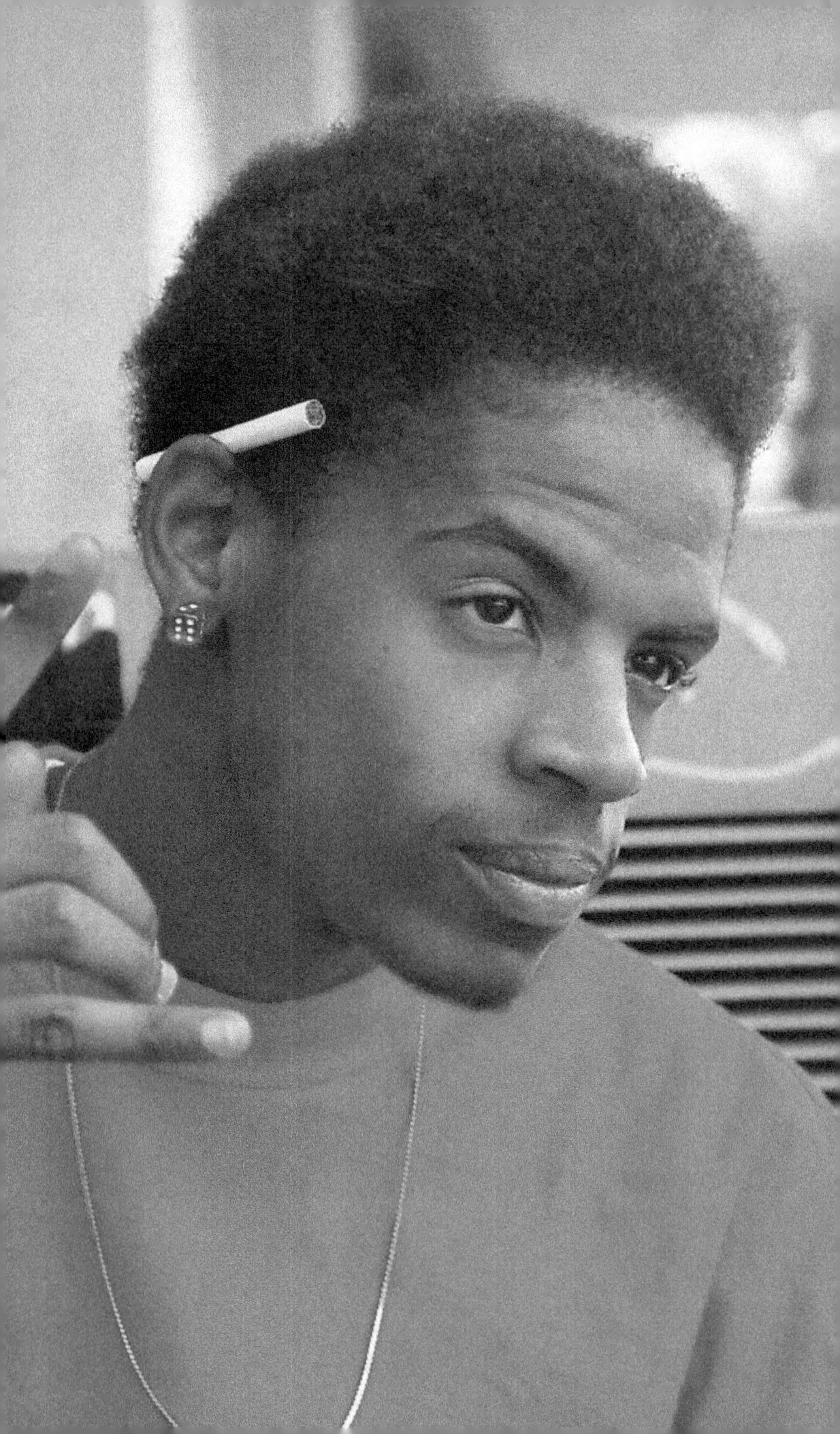

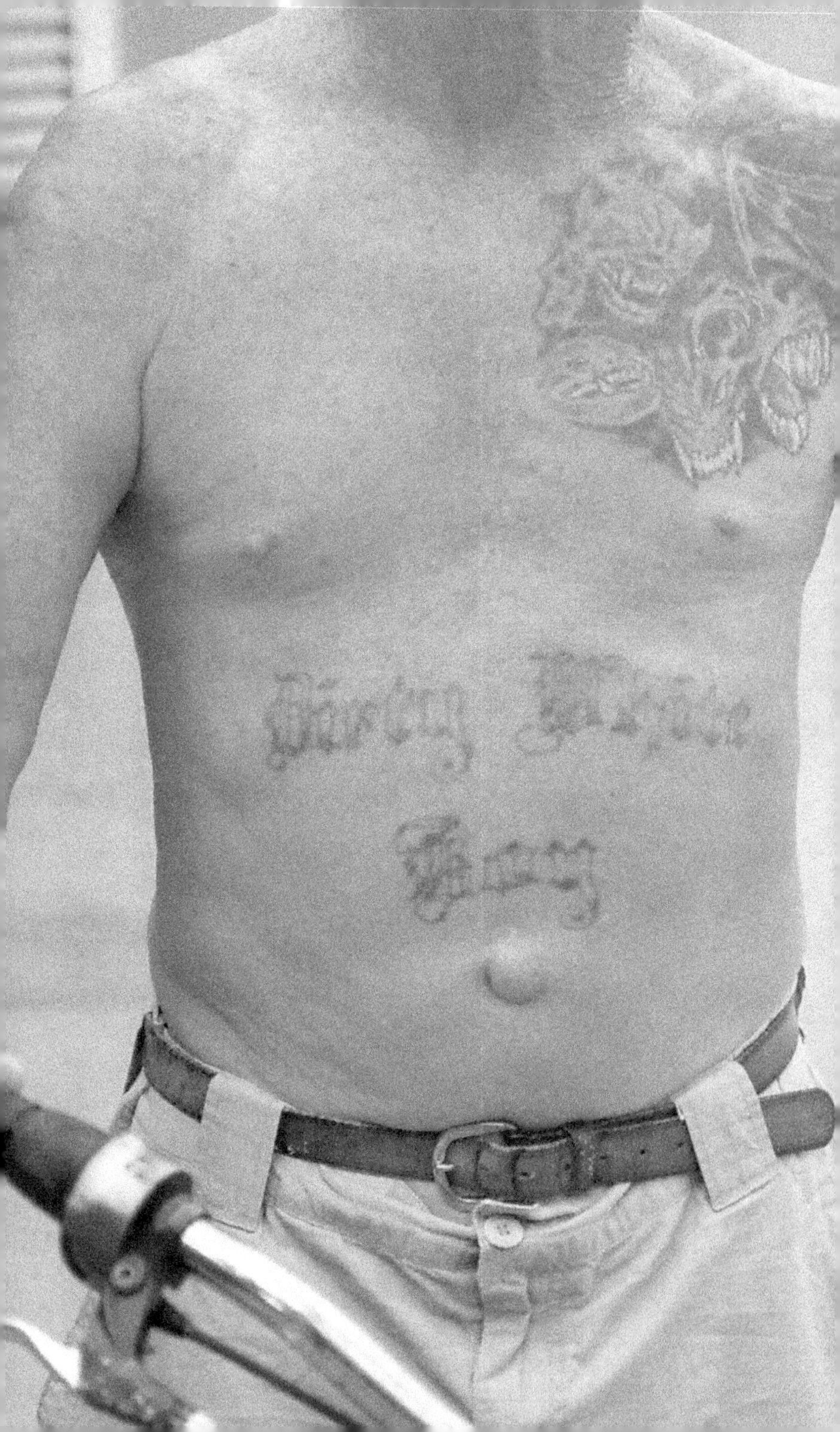
Dirty

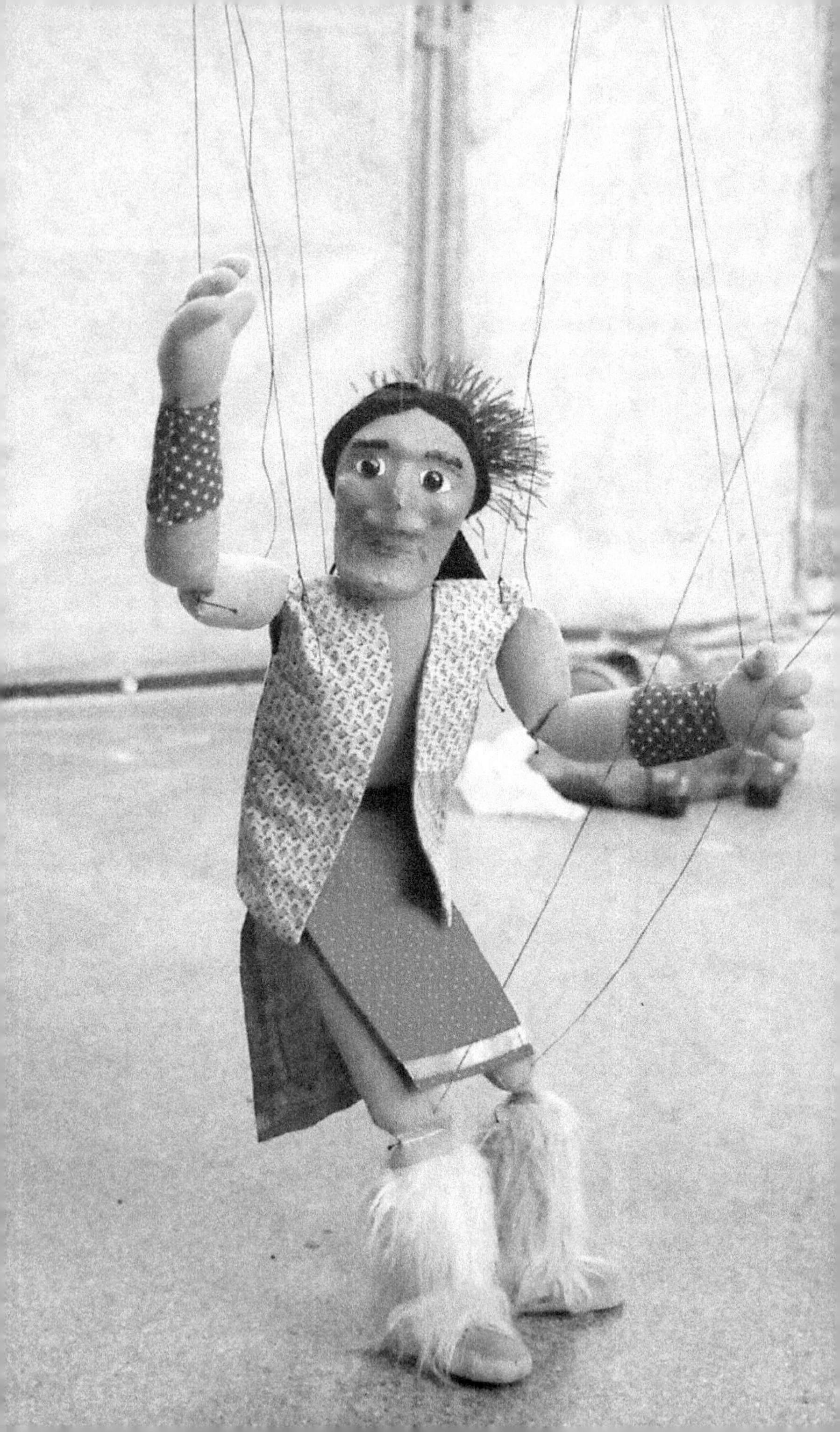

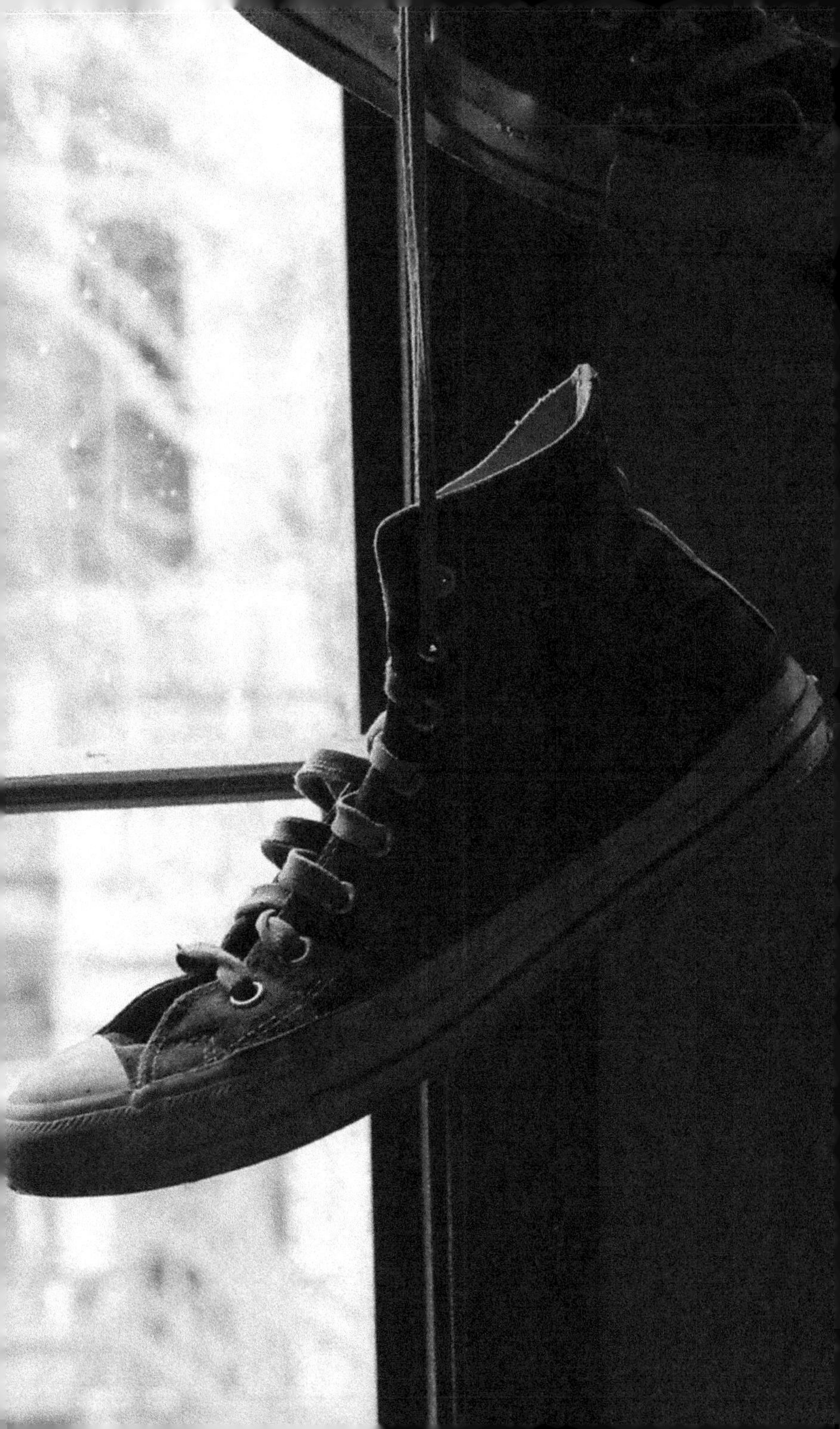

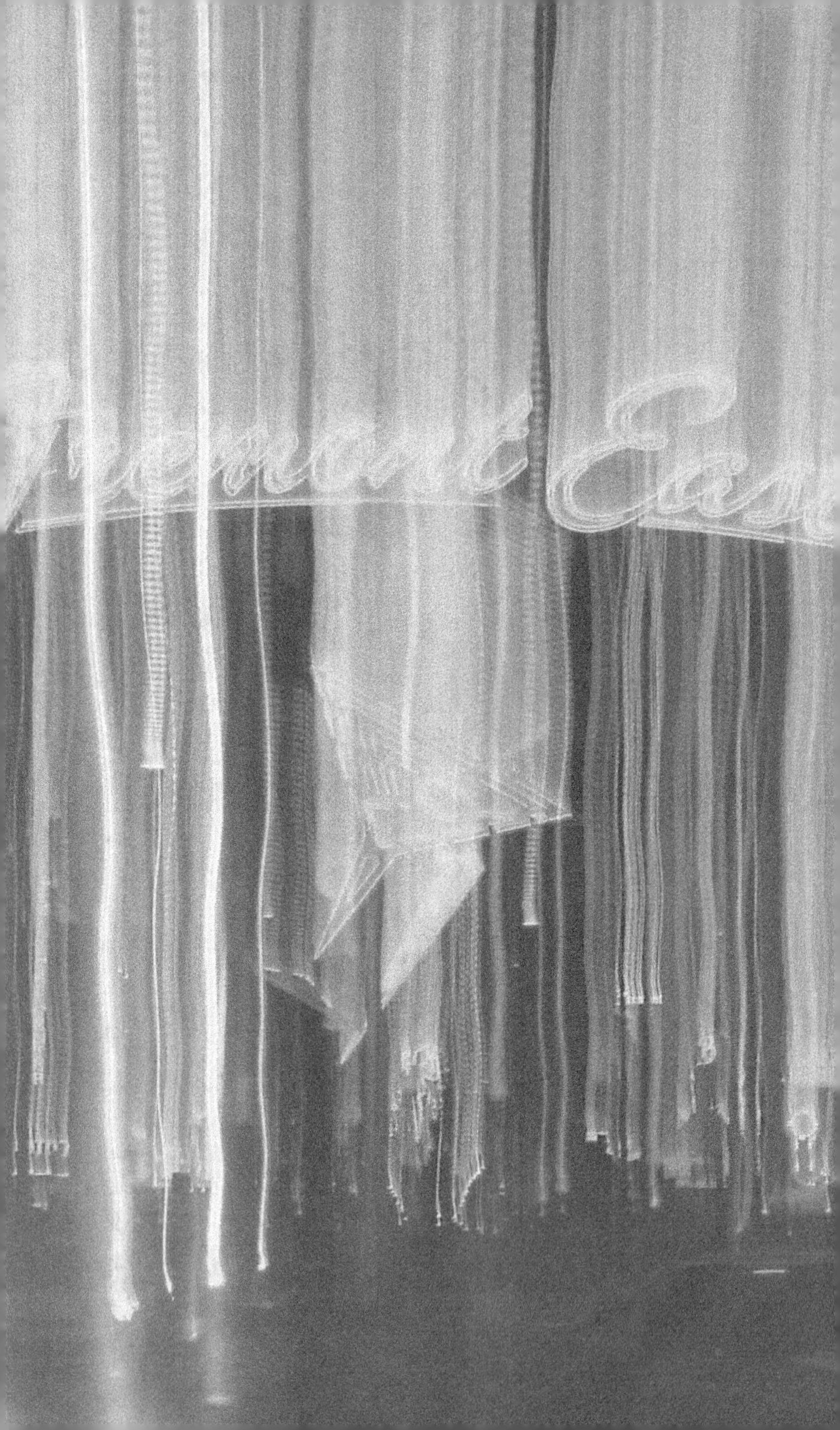

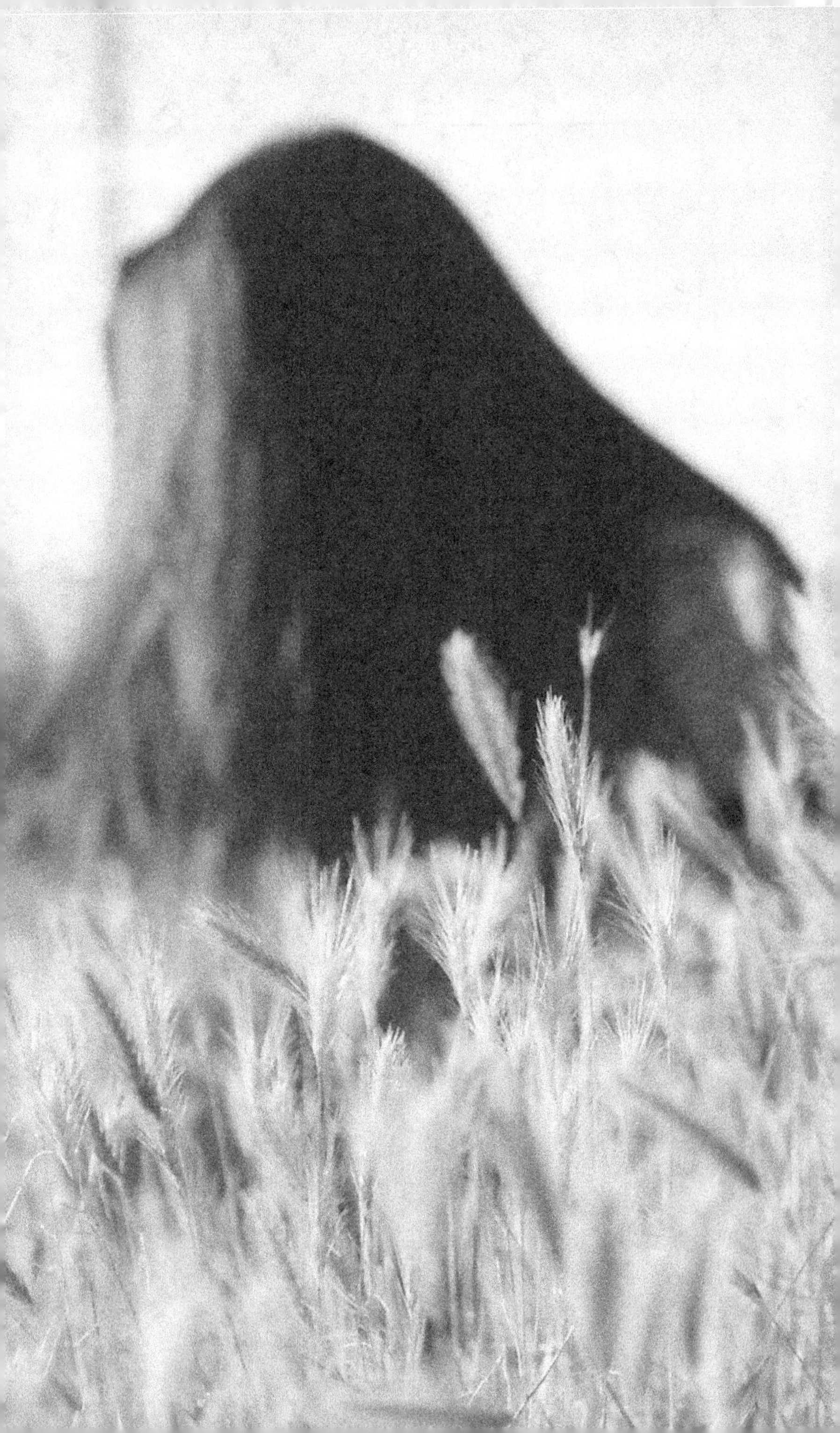

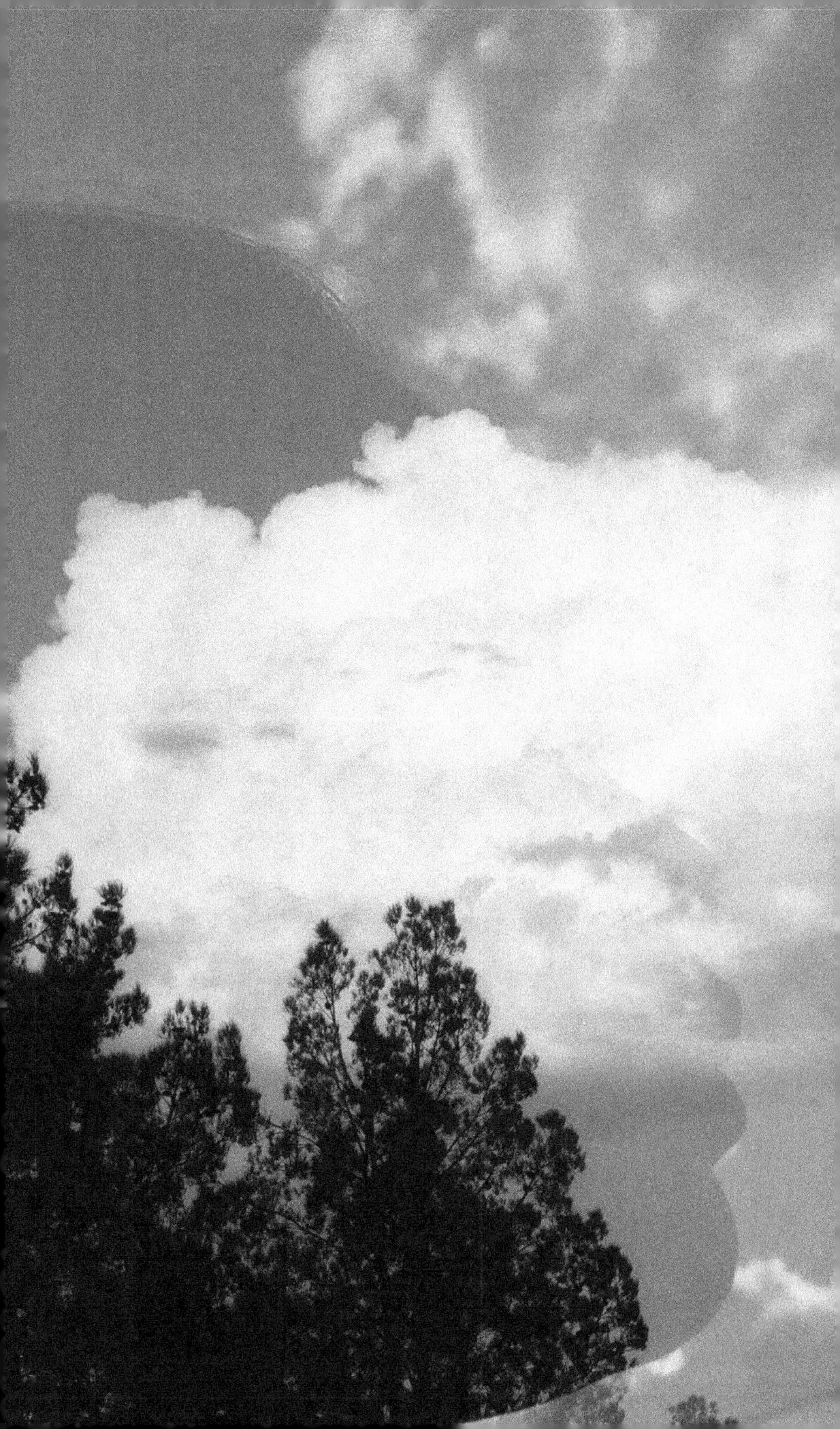

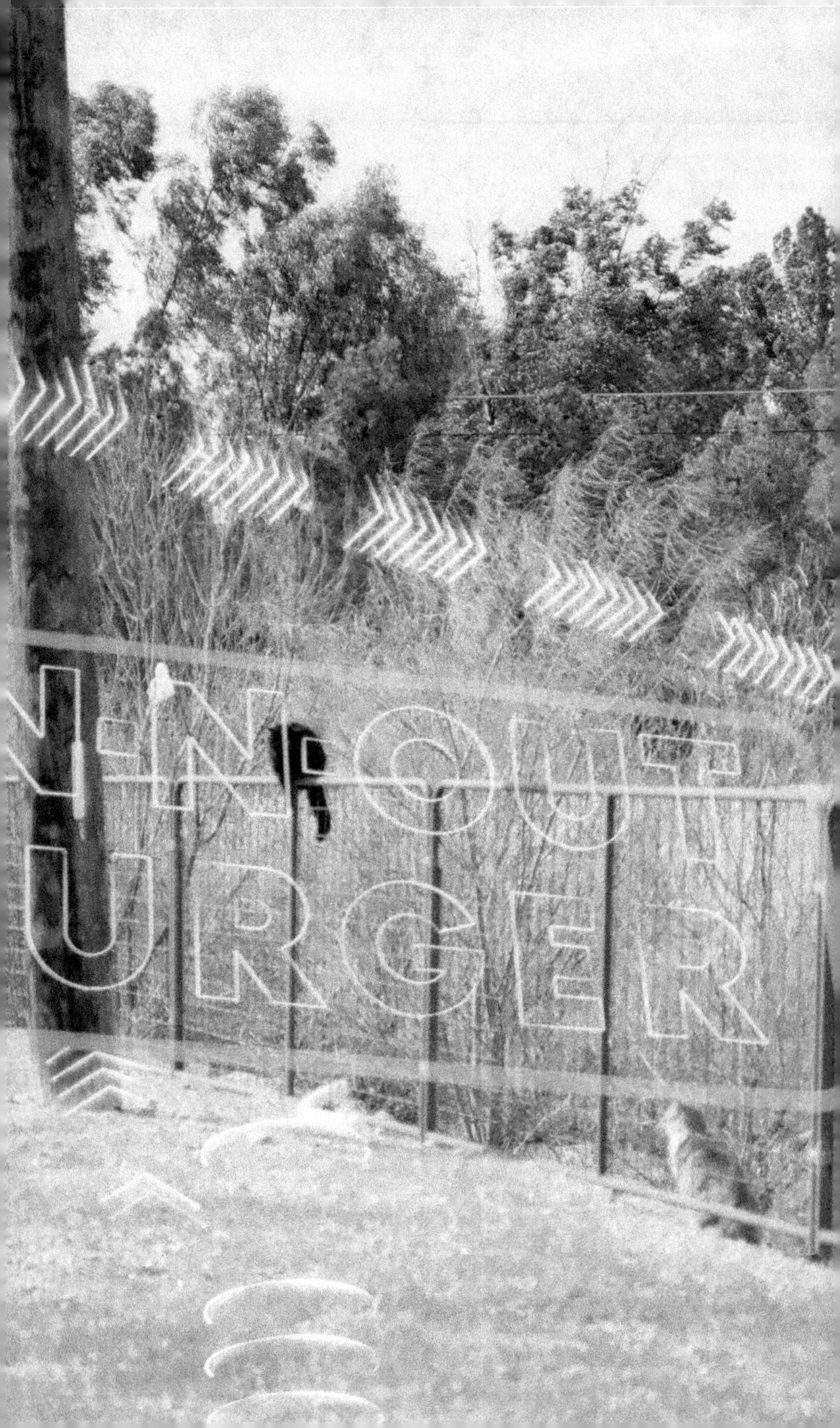
N-OUT
URGER

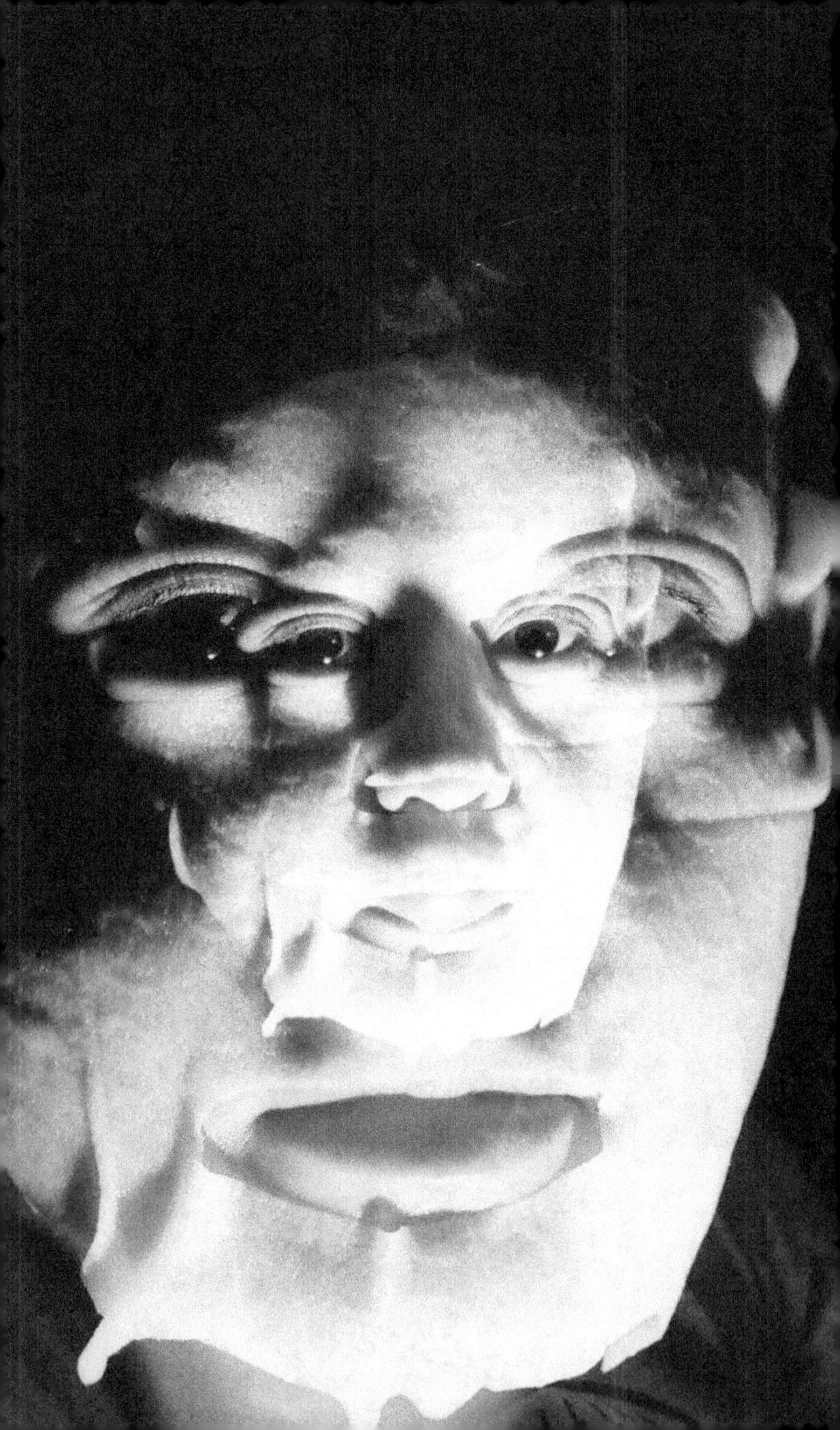

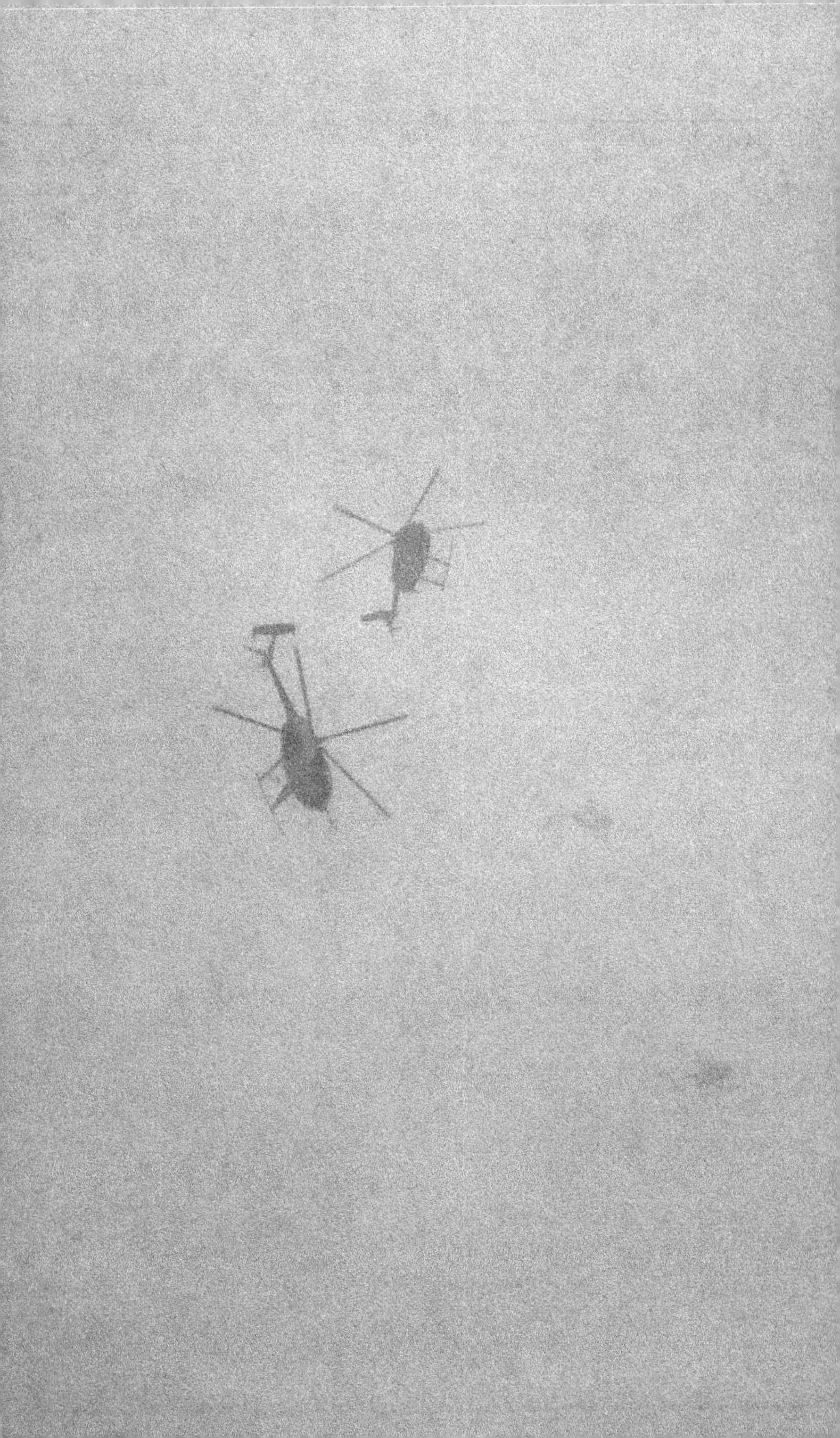

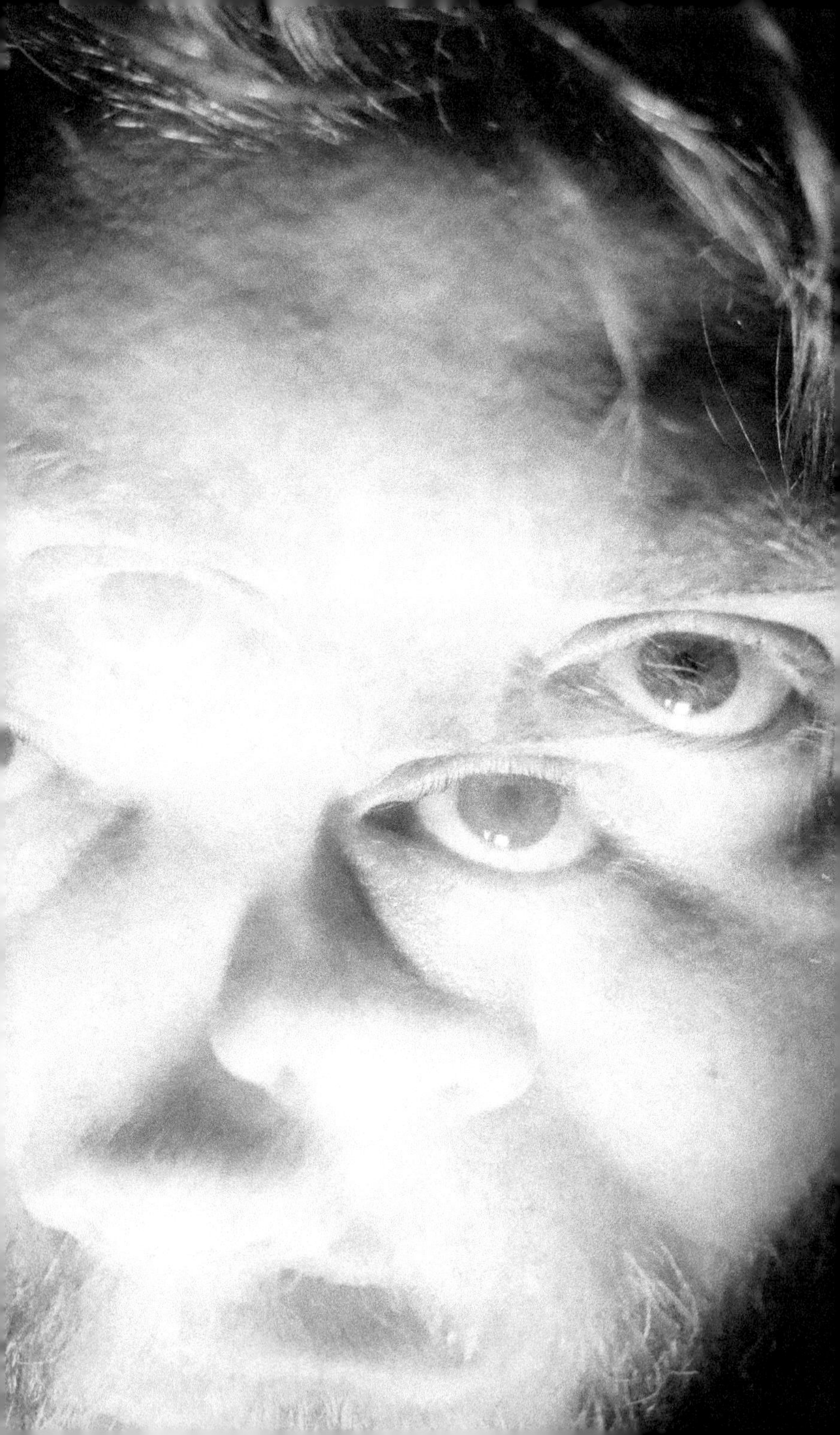

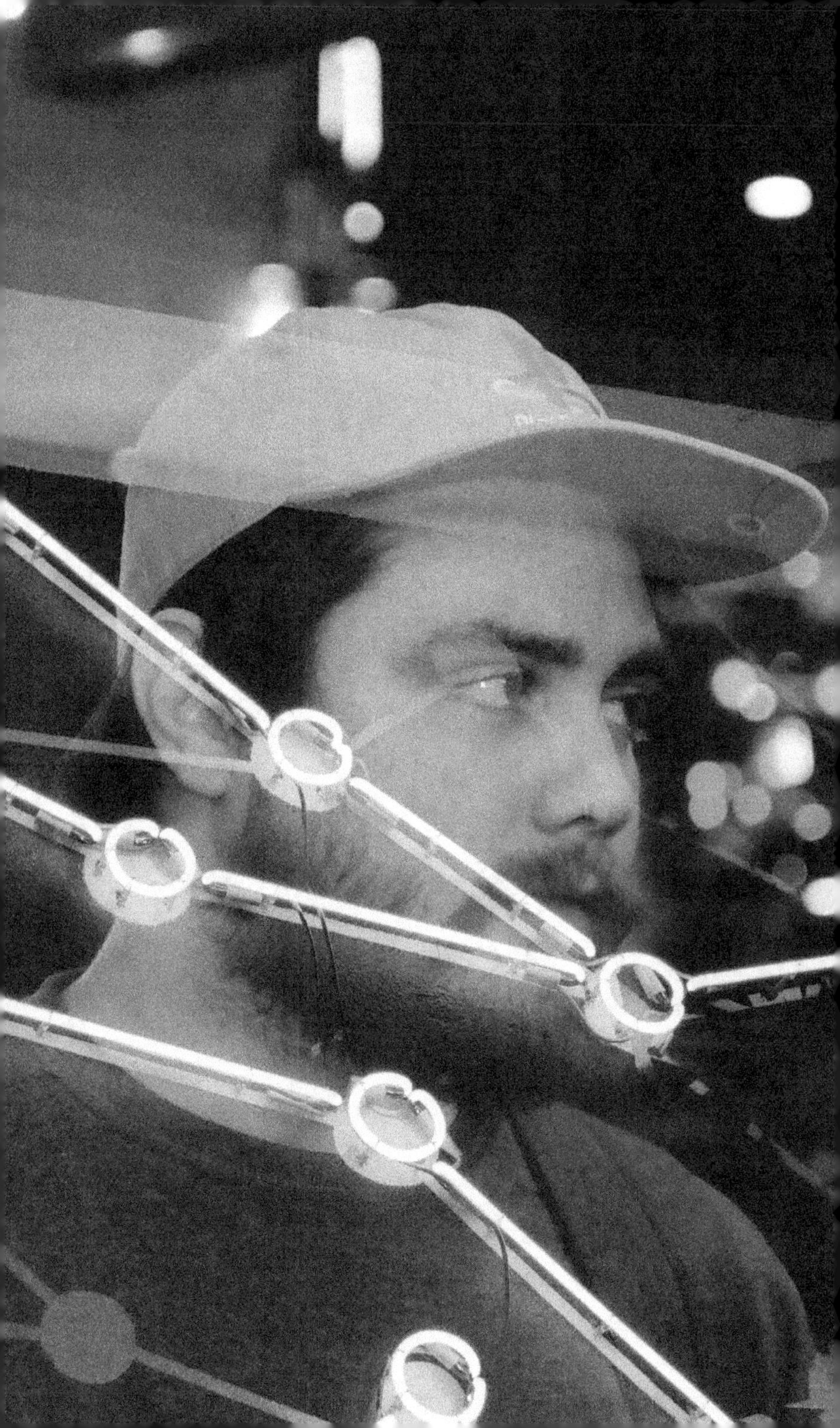

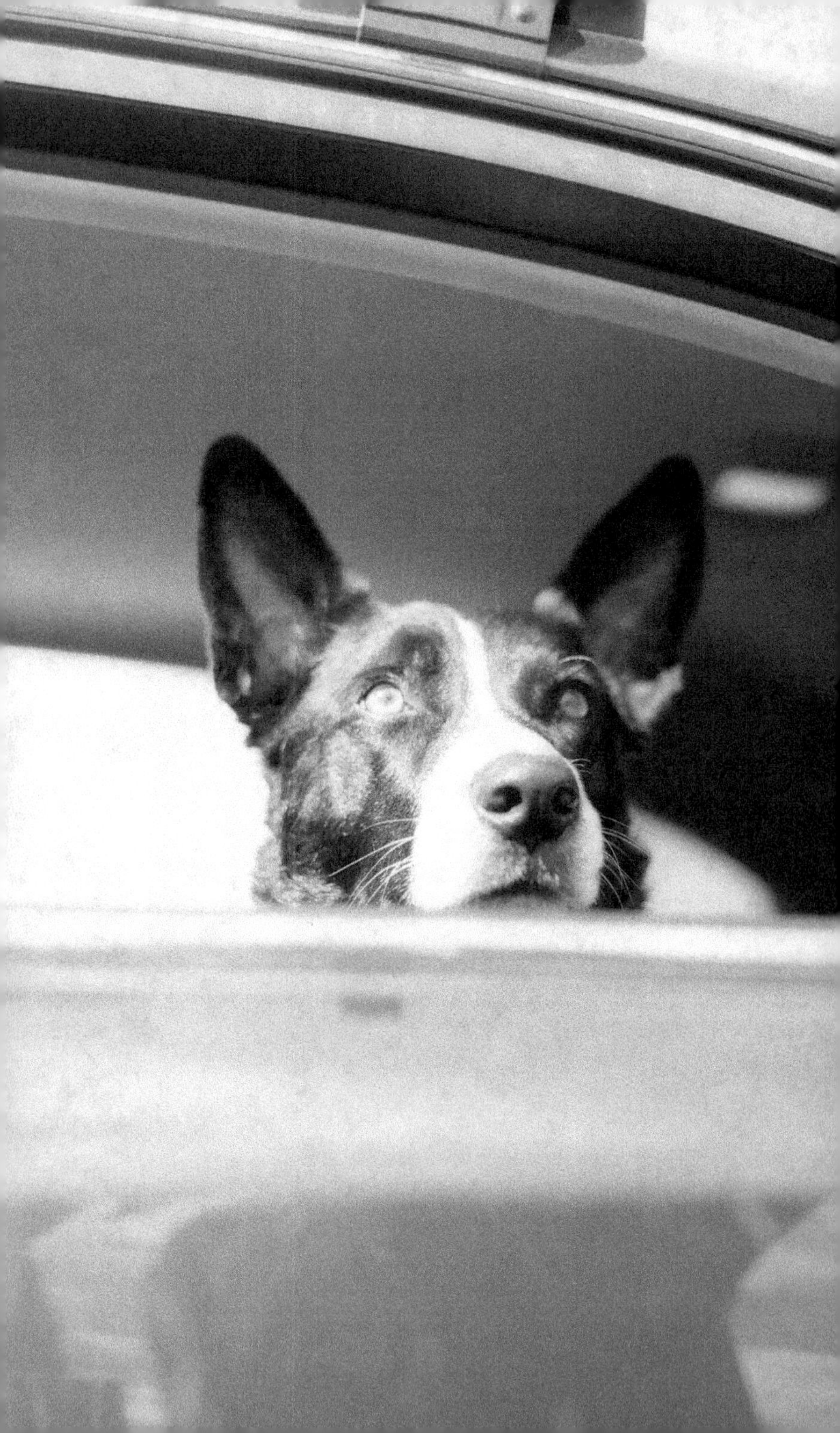

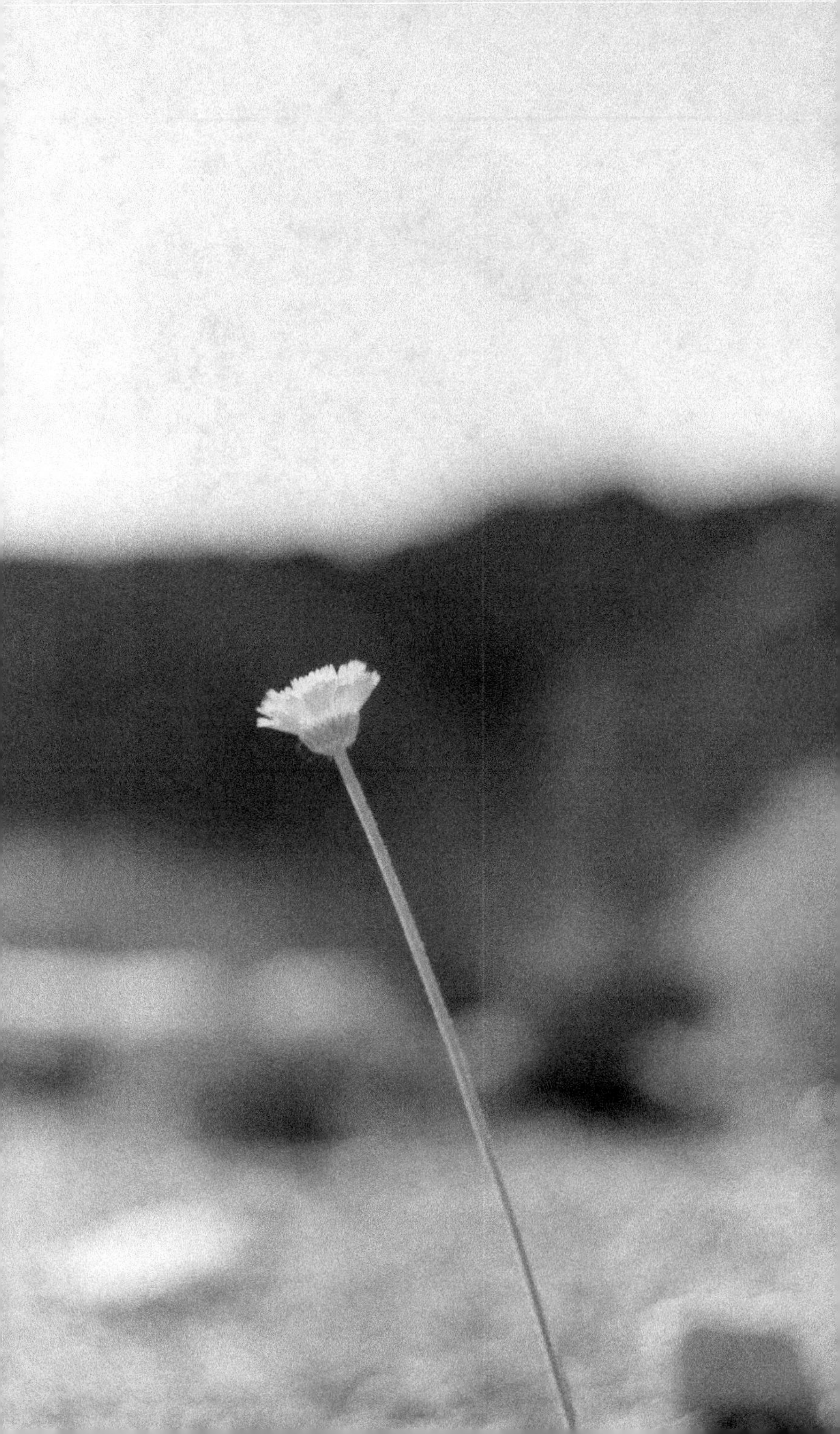

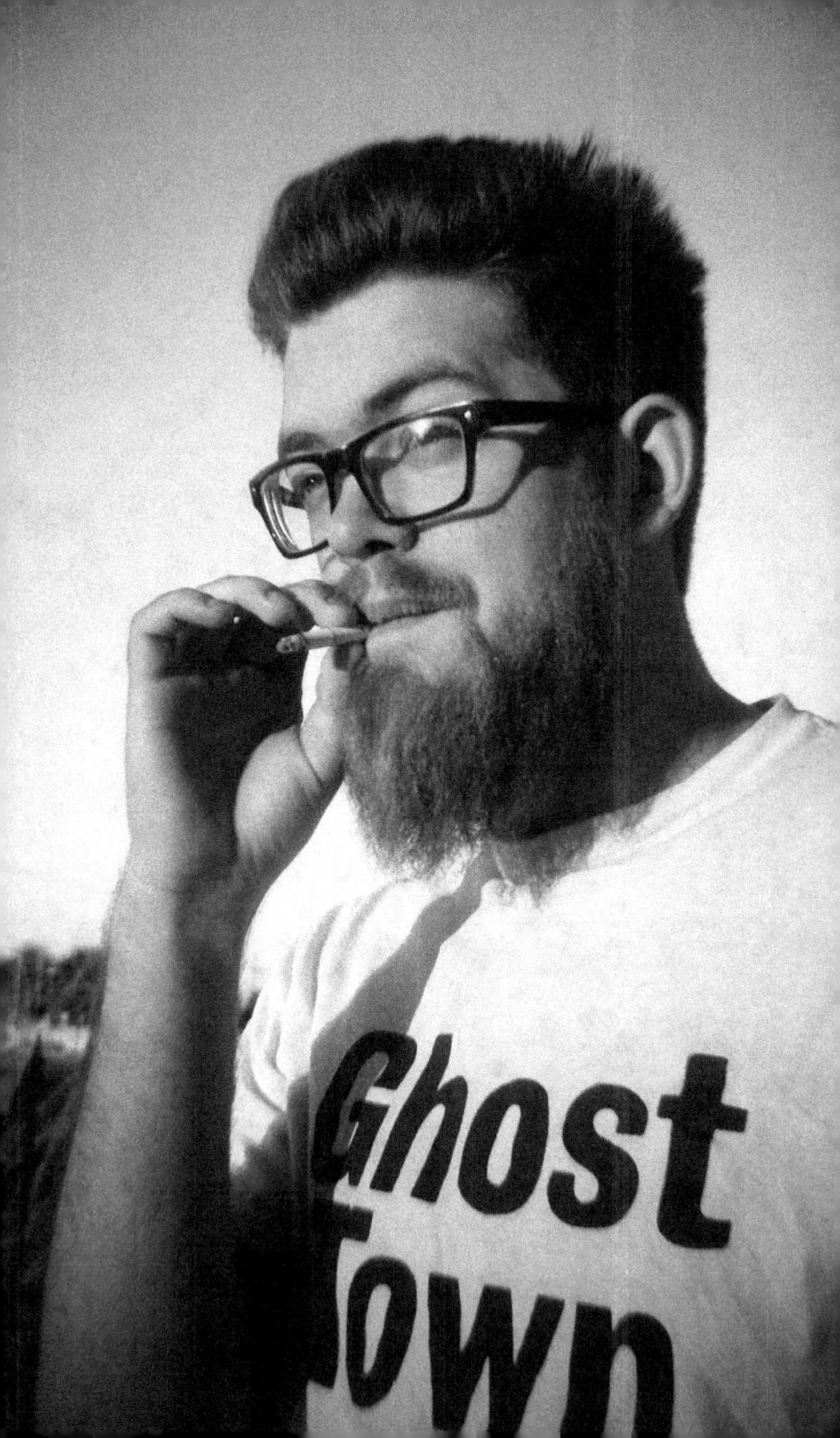
Ghost

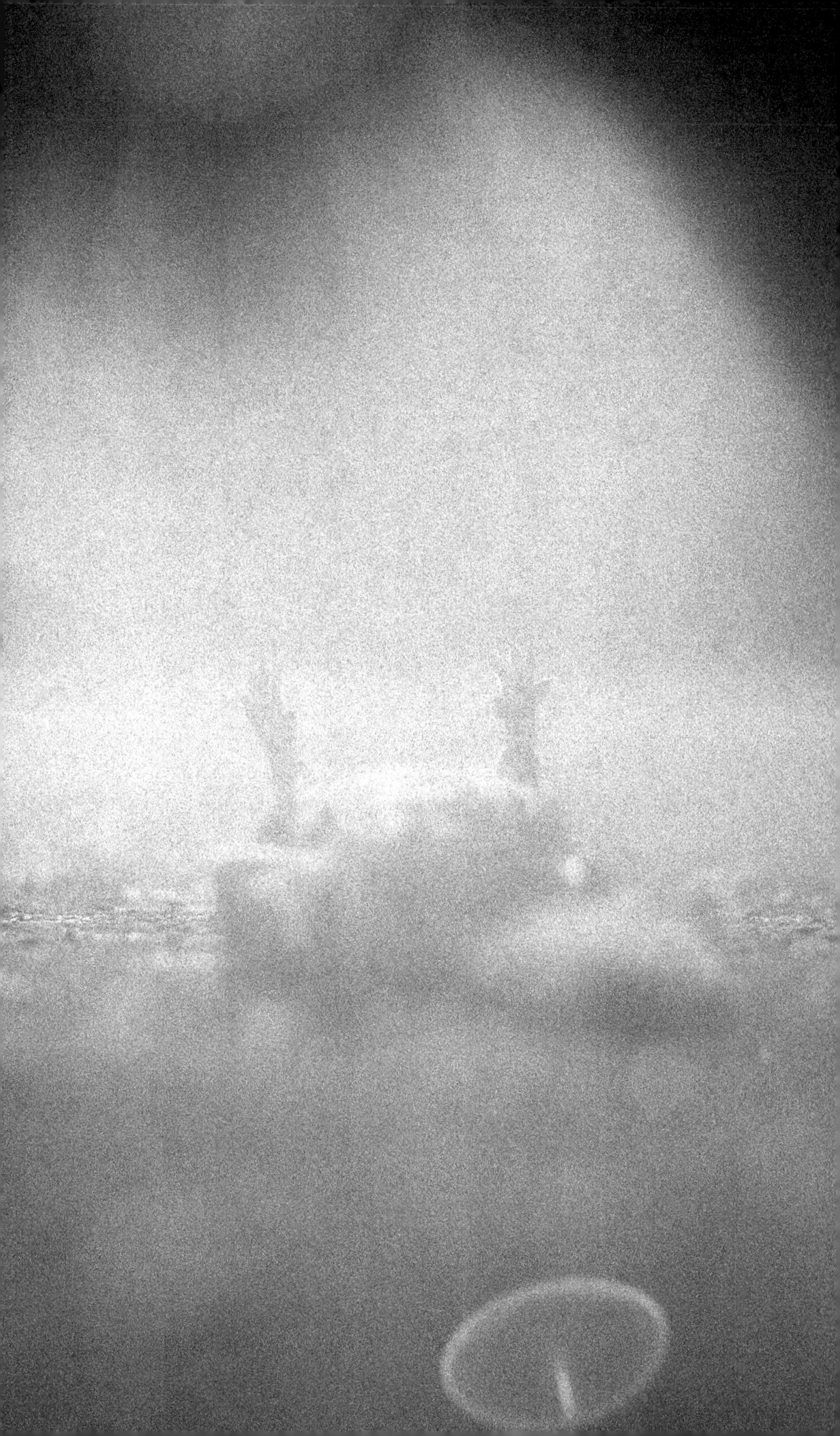

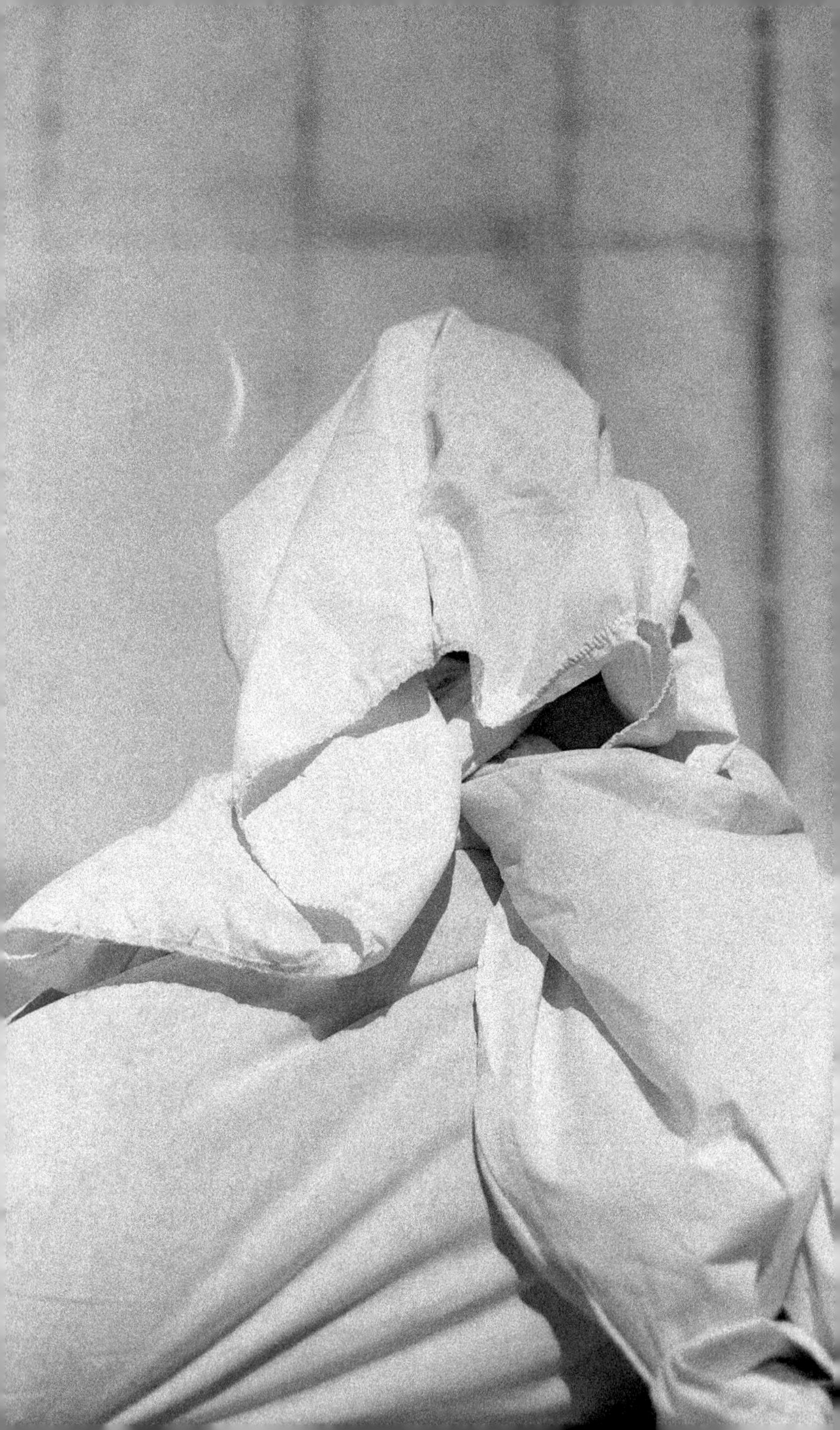

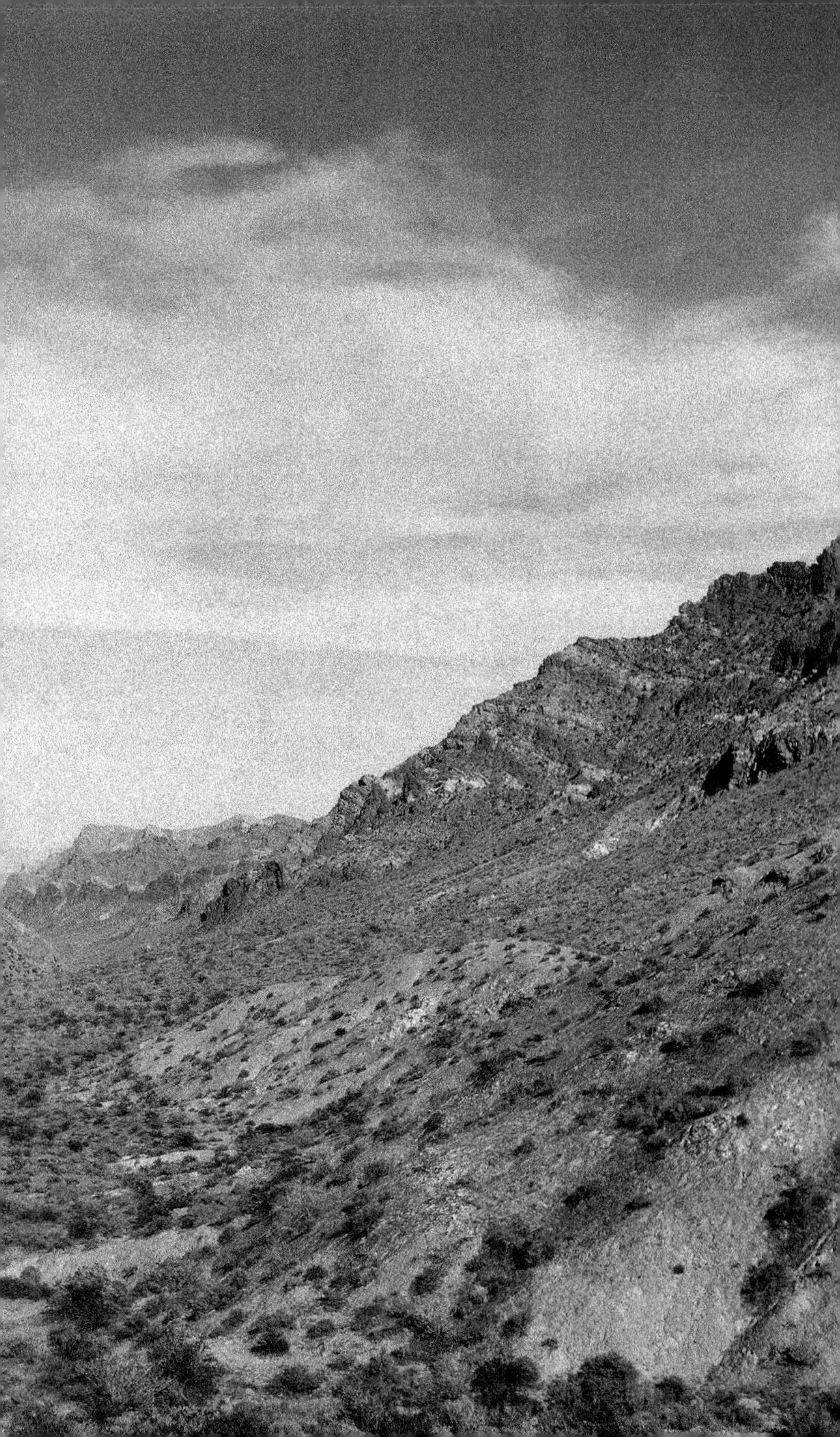

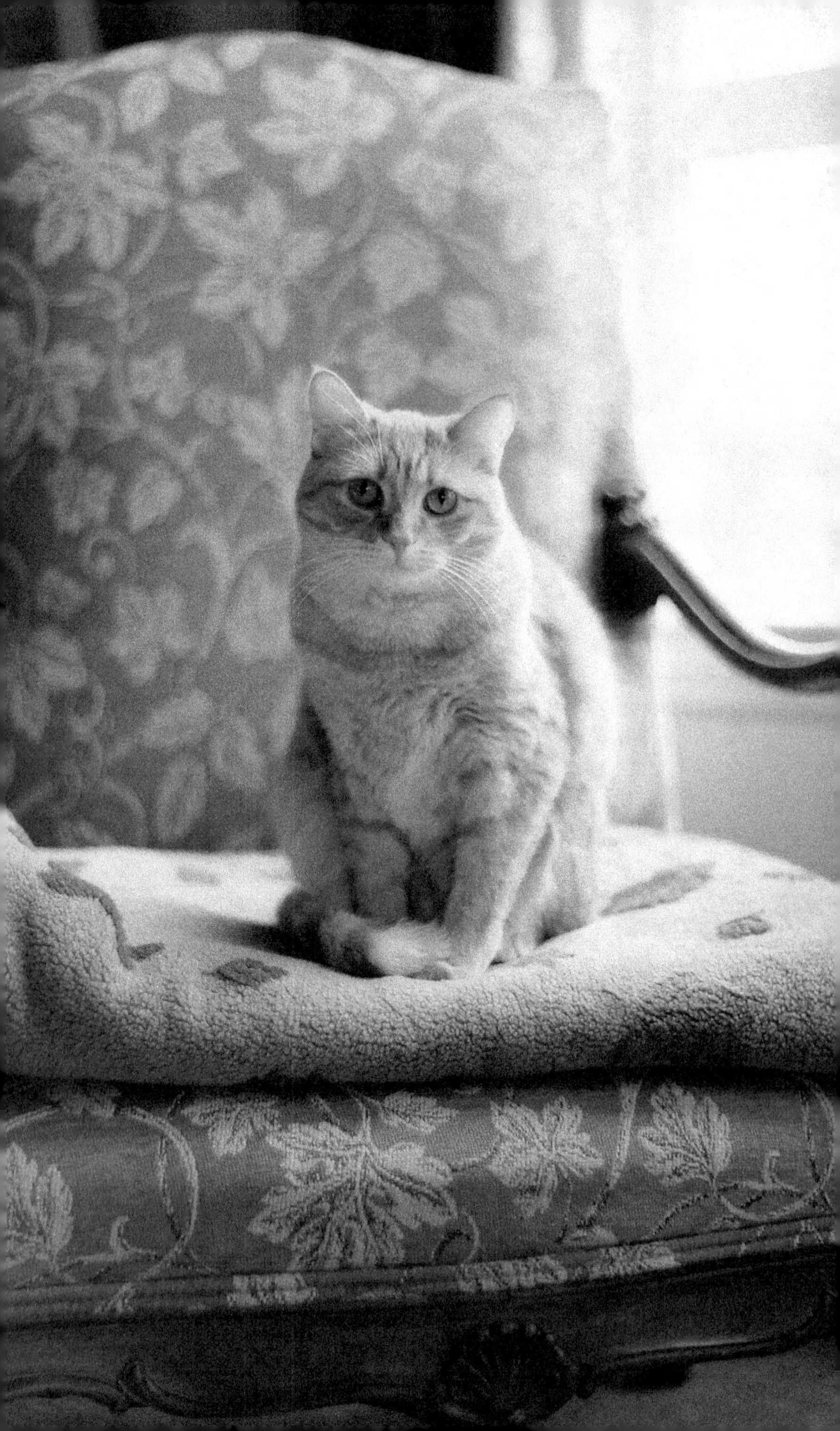

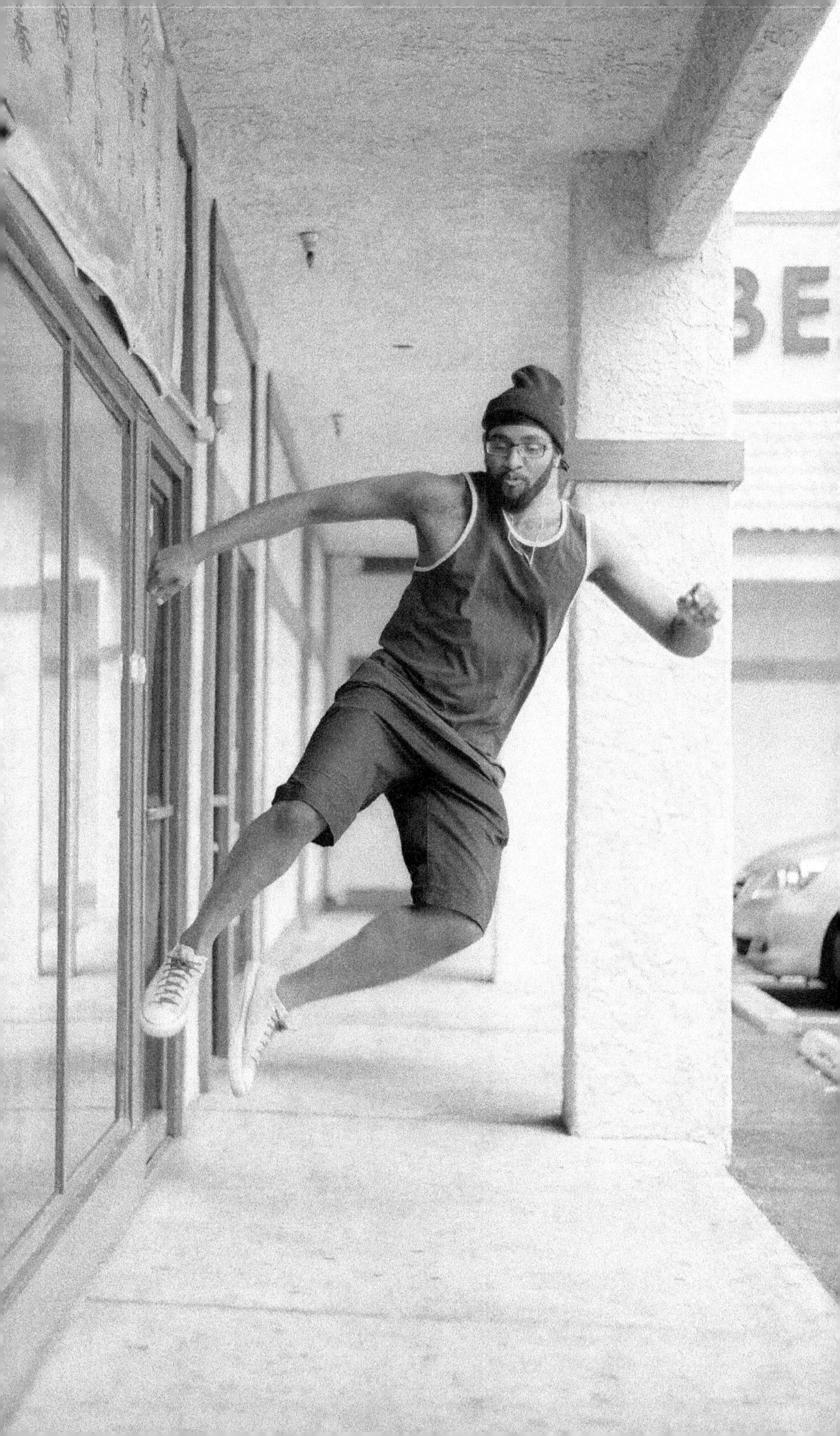

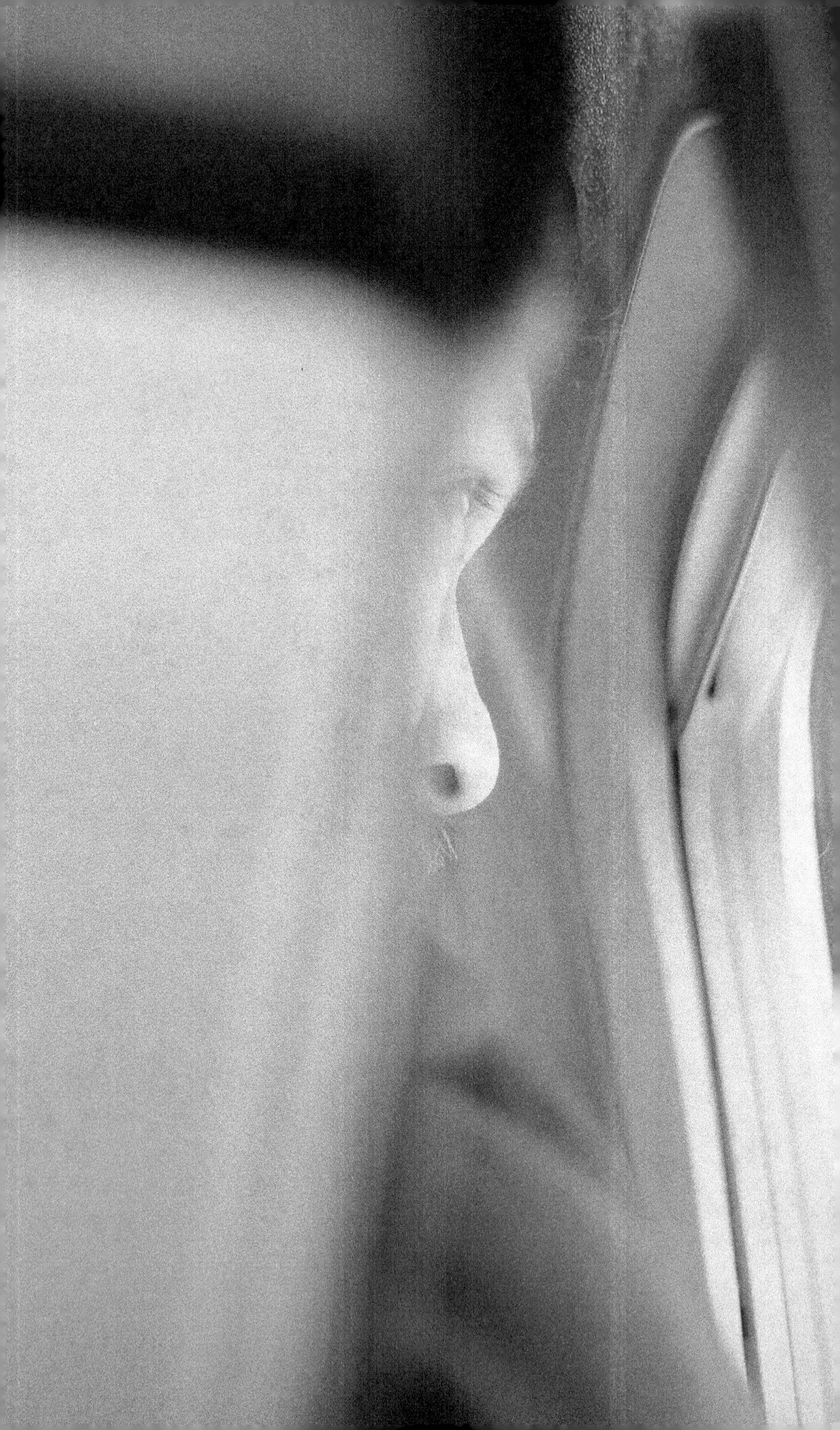

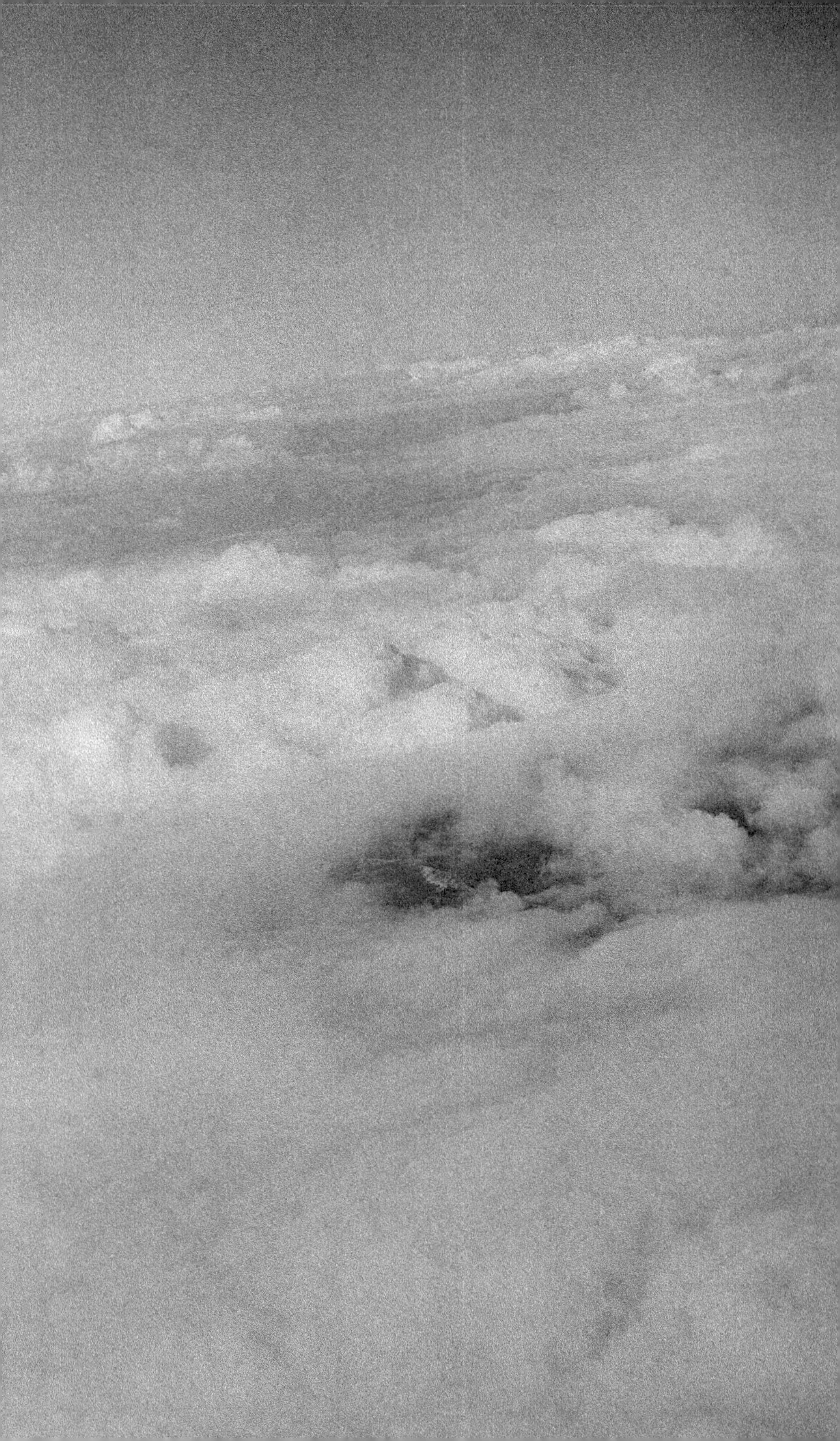

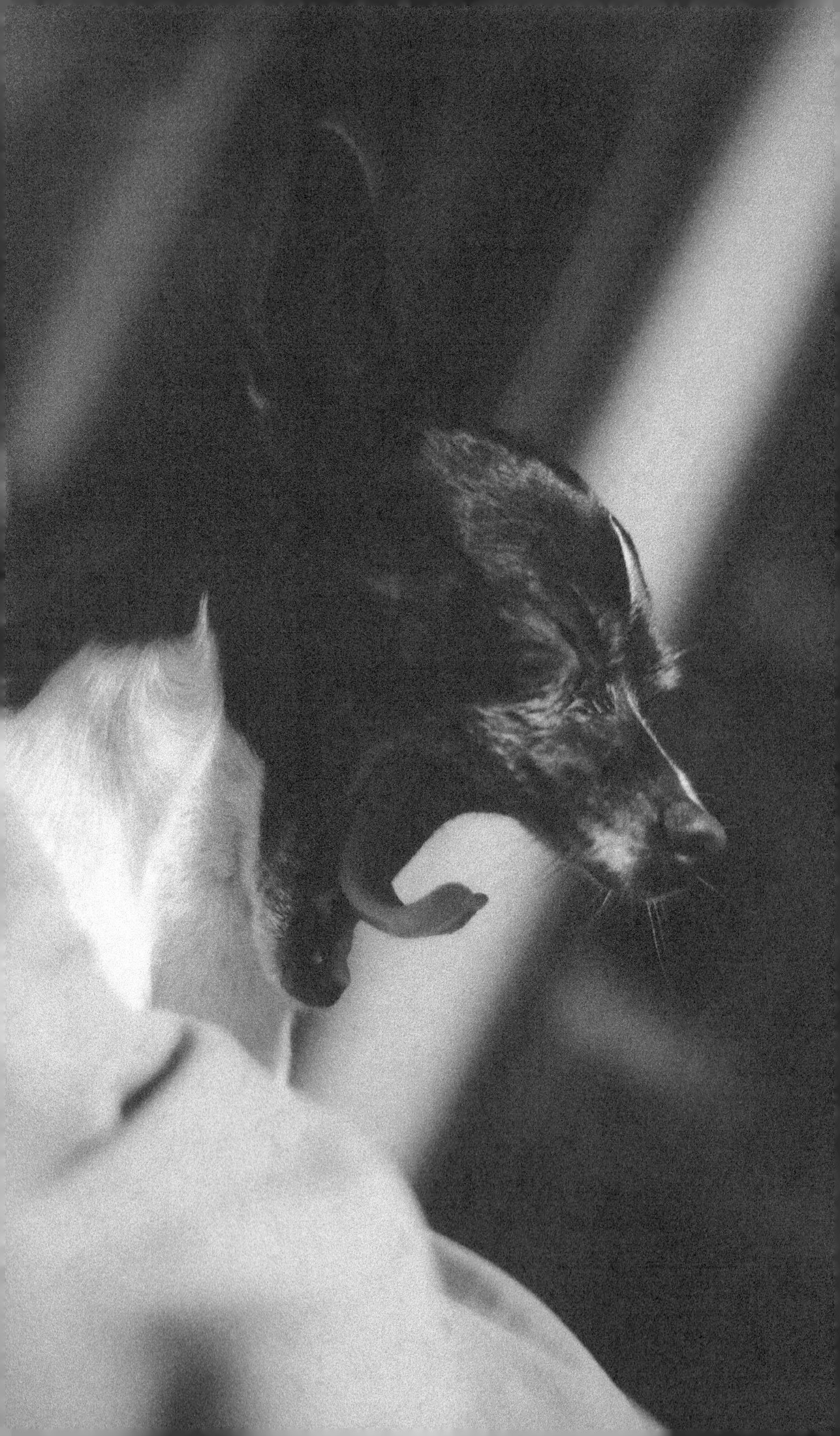

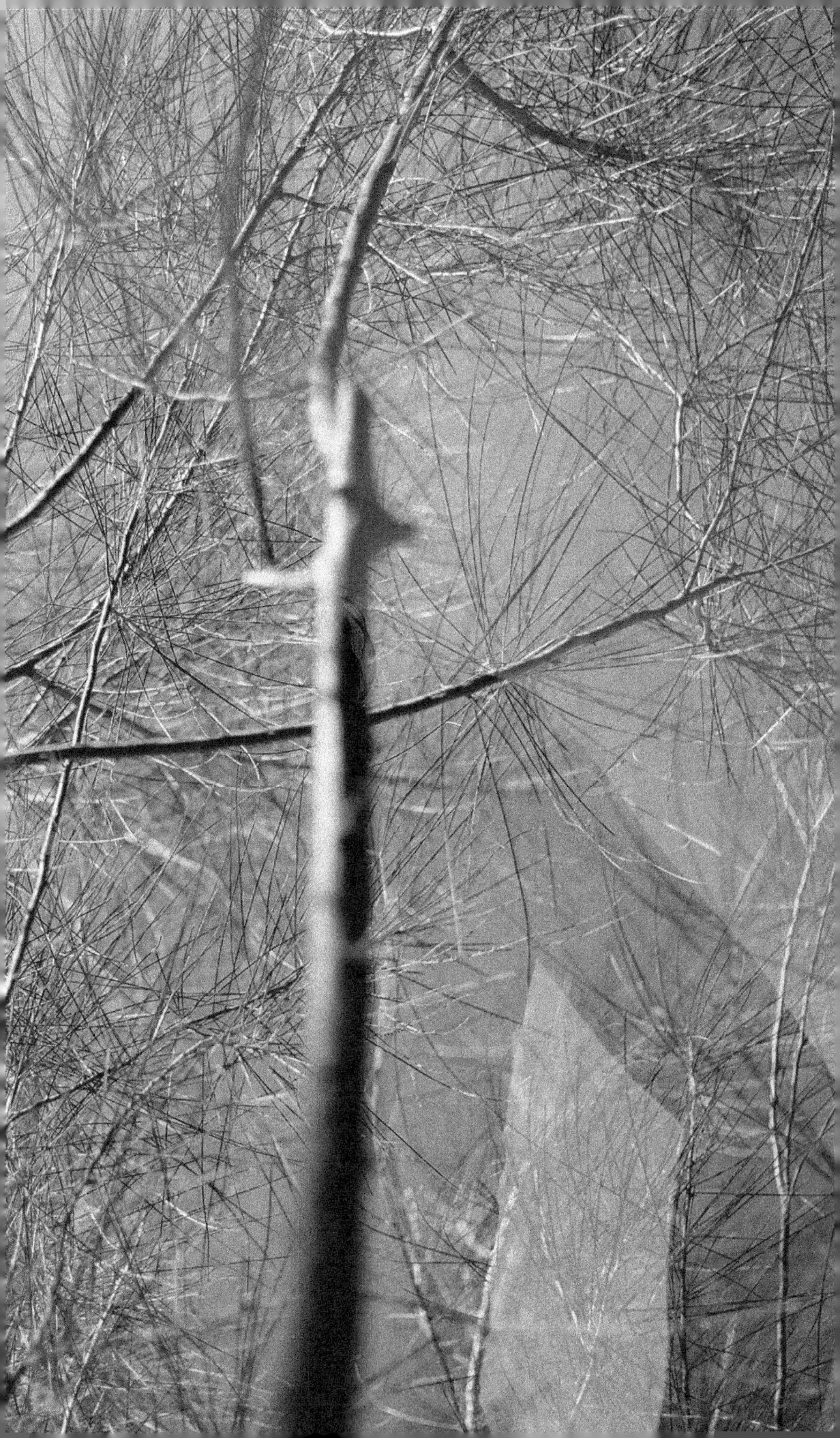

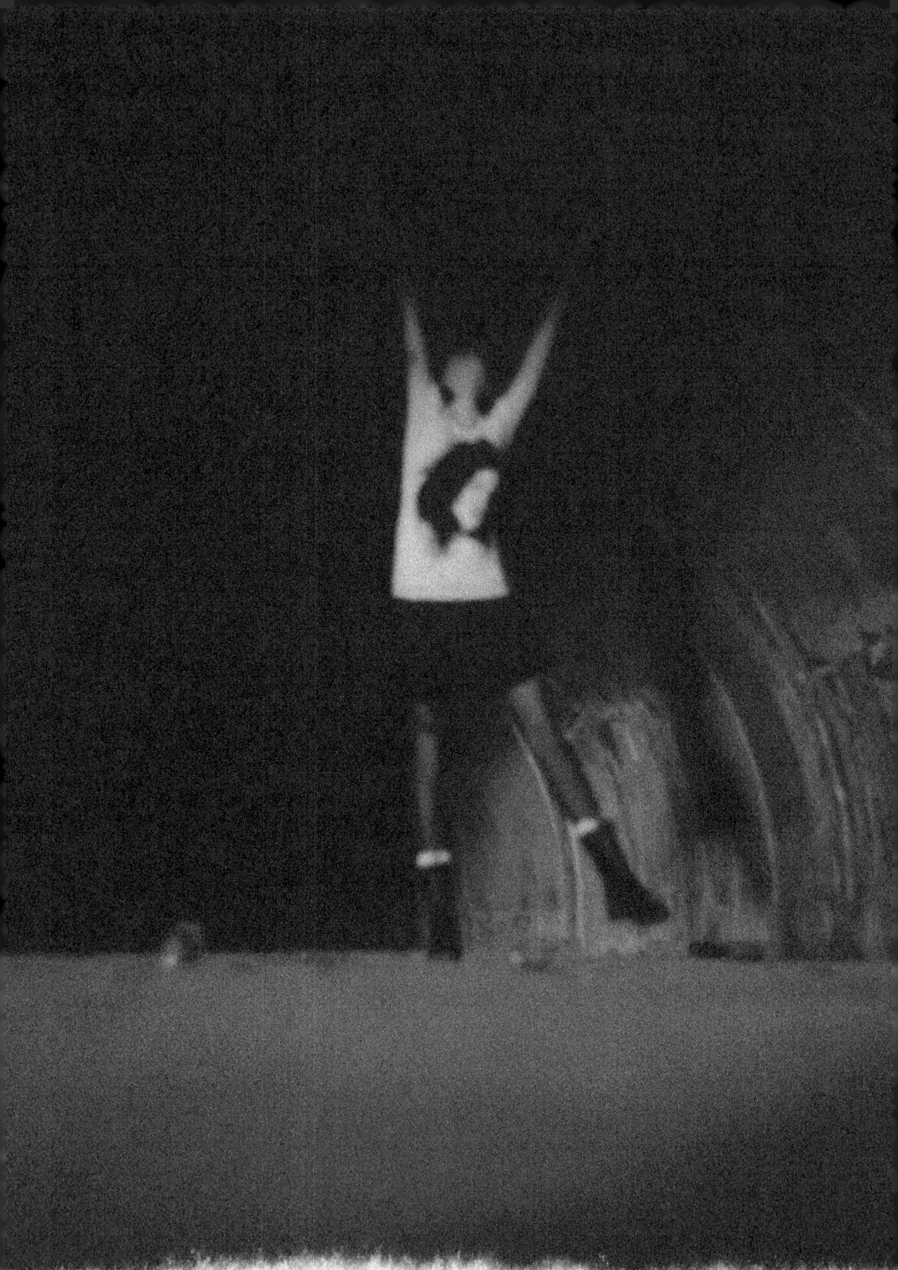

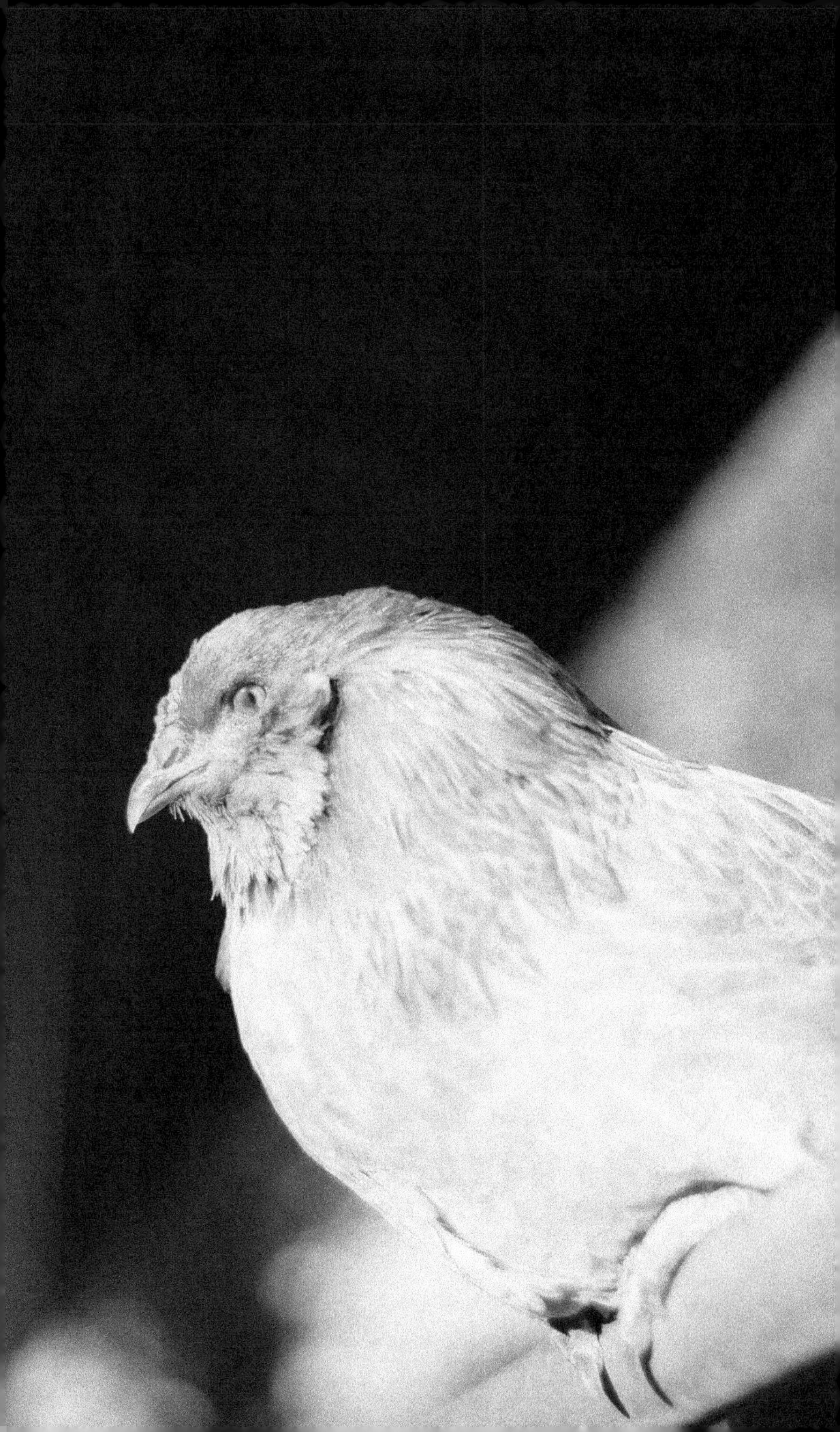

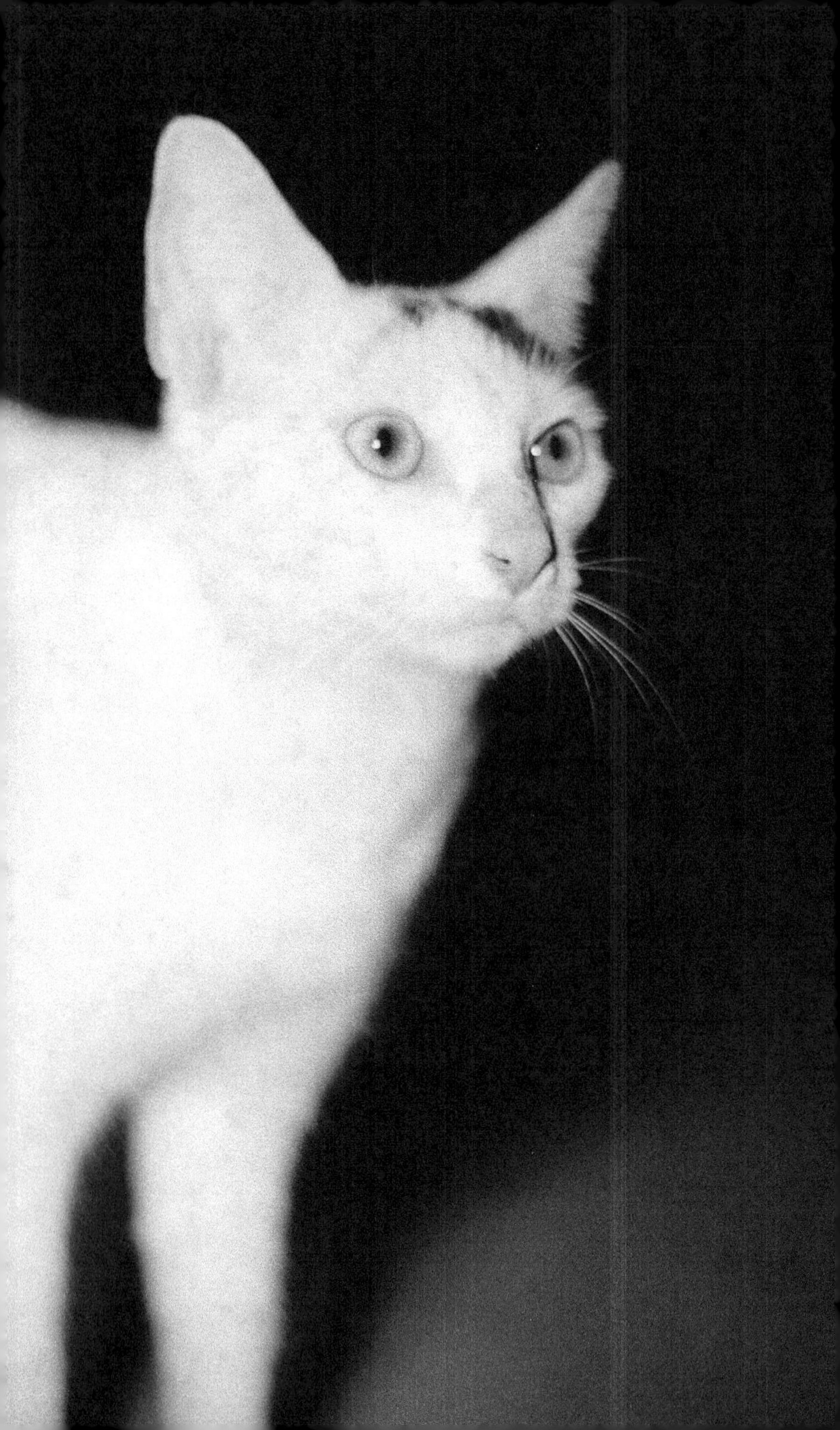

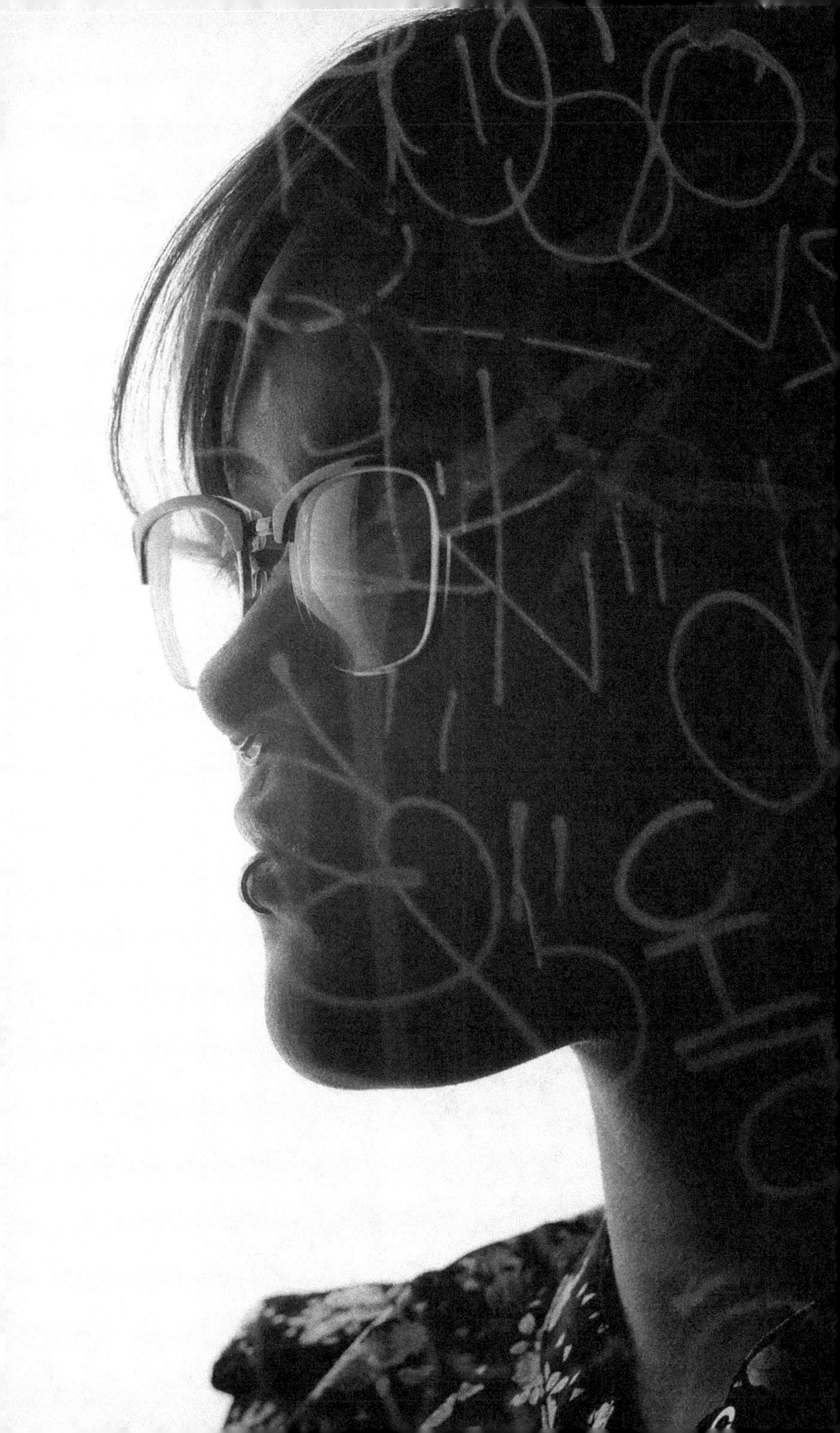

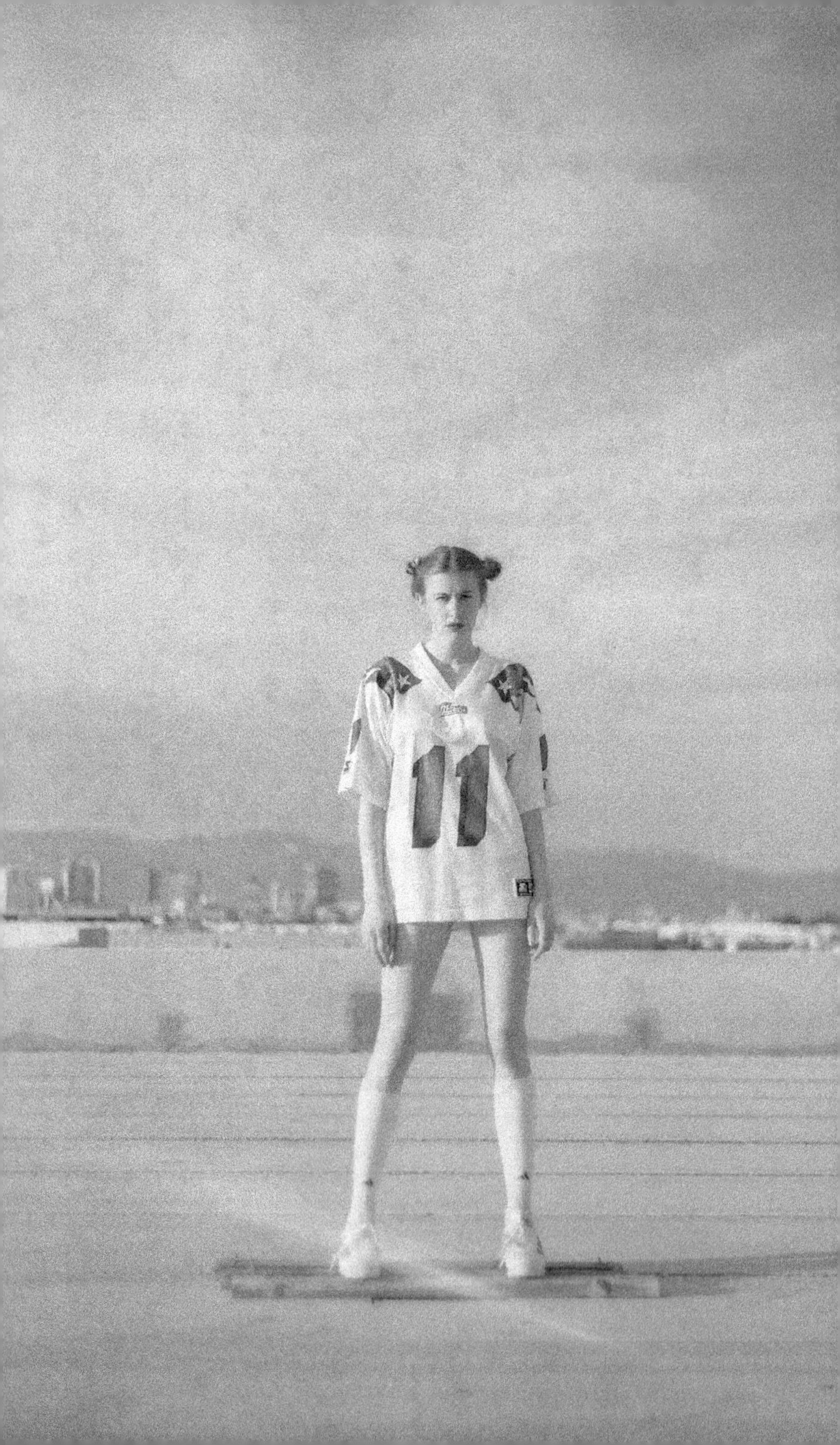
11

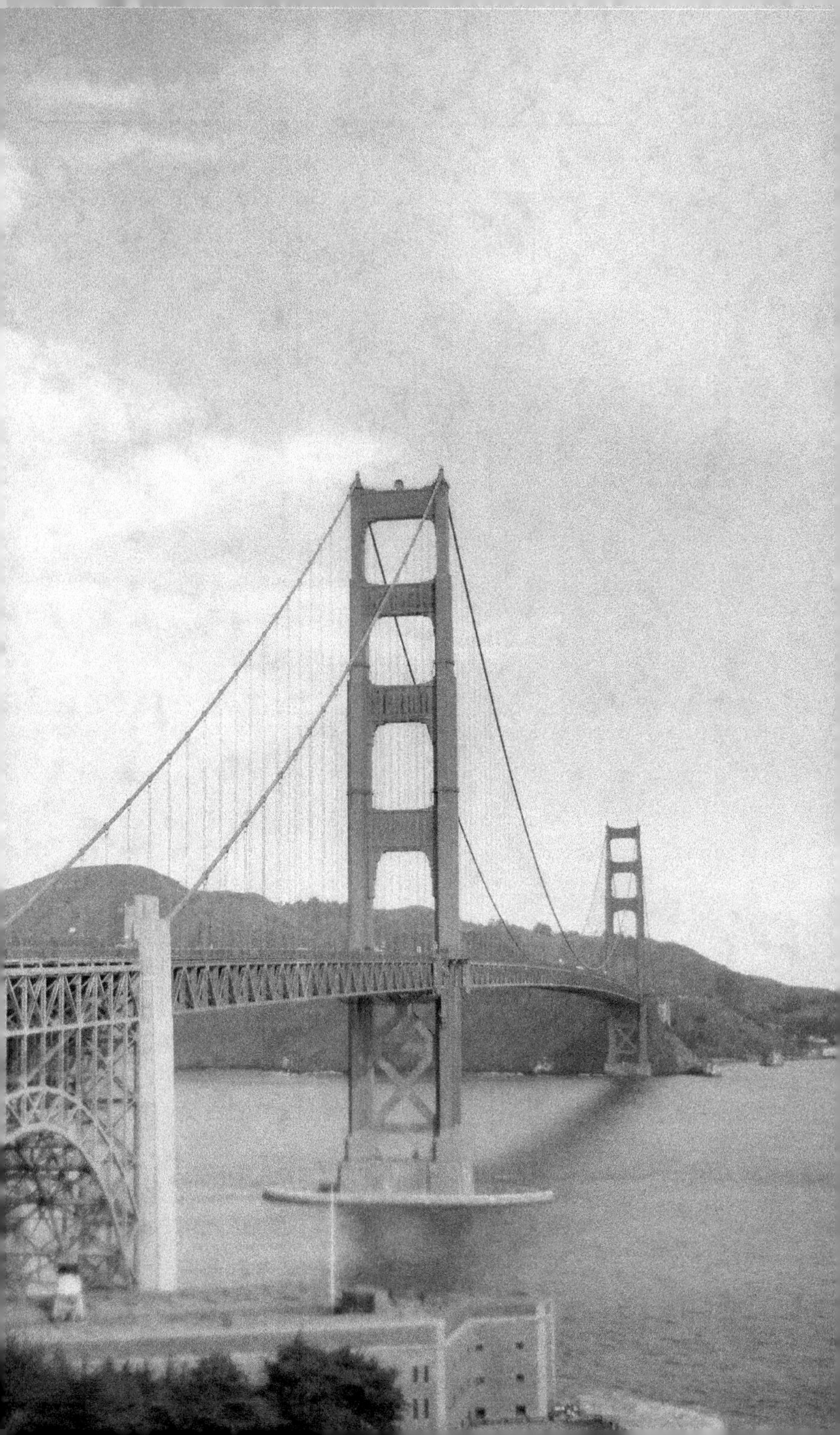

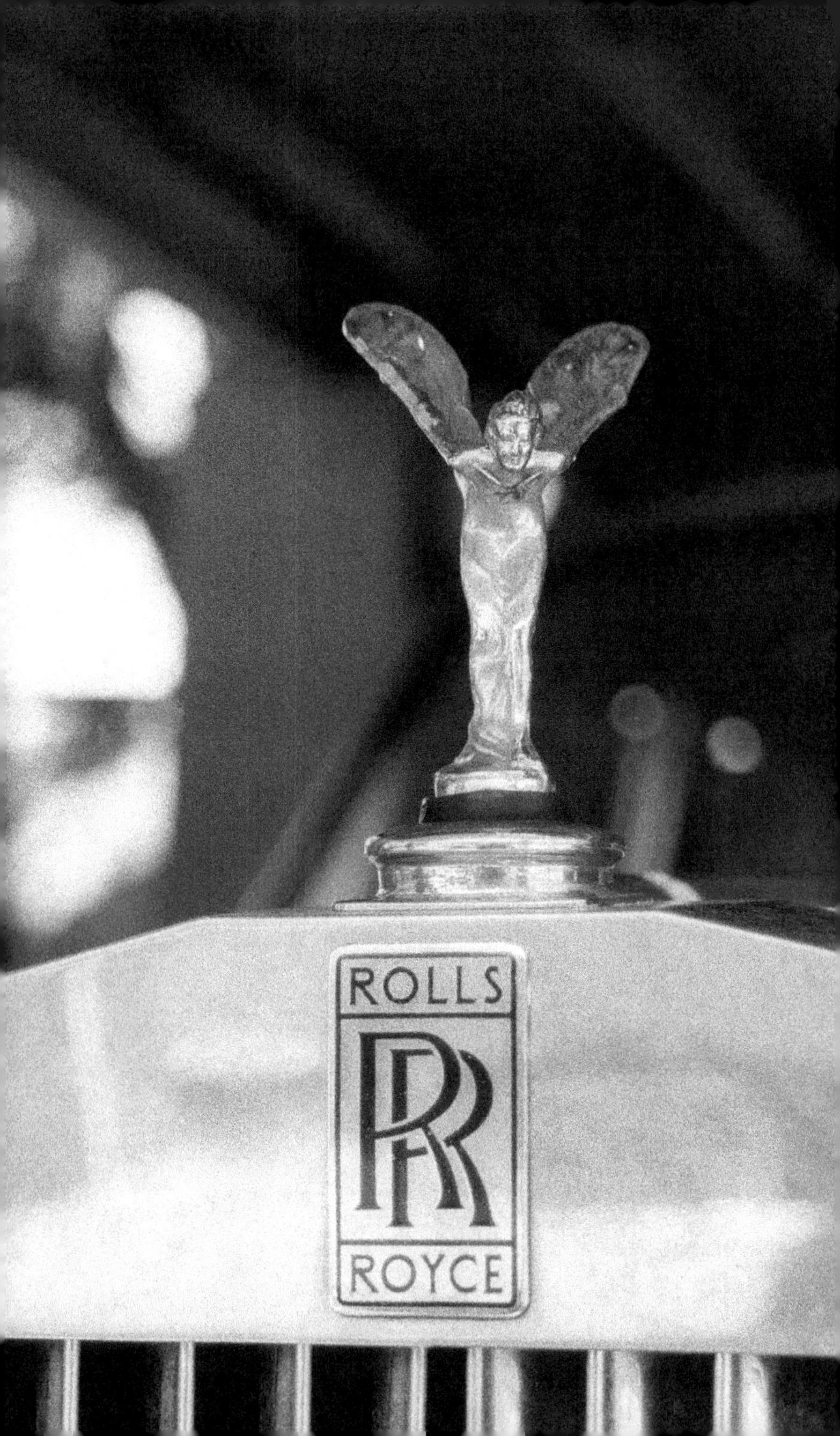
ROLLS
ROYCE

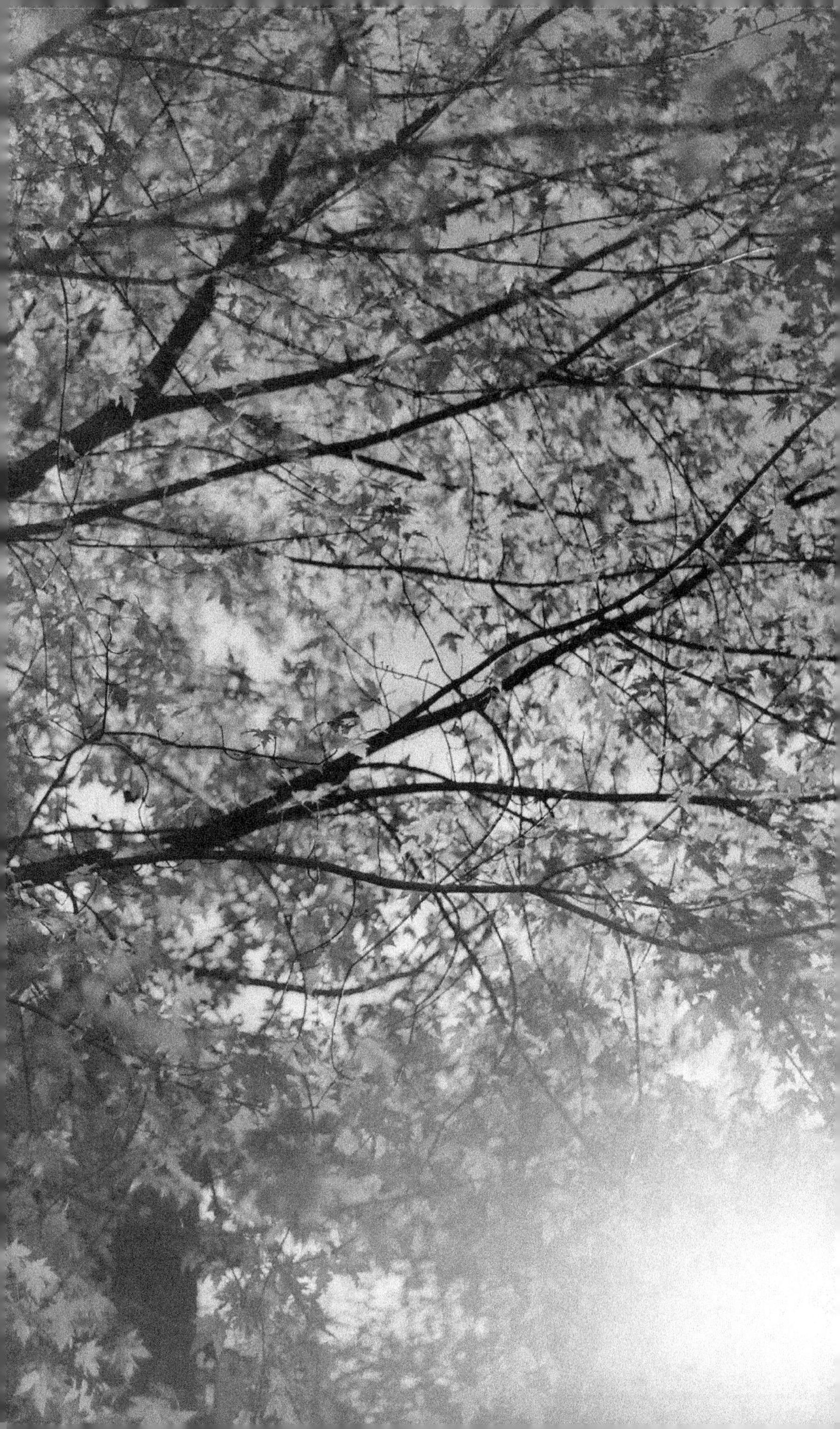

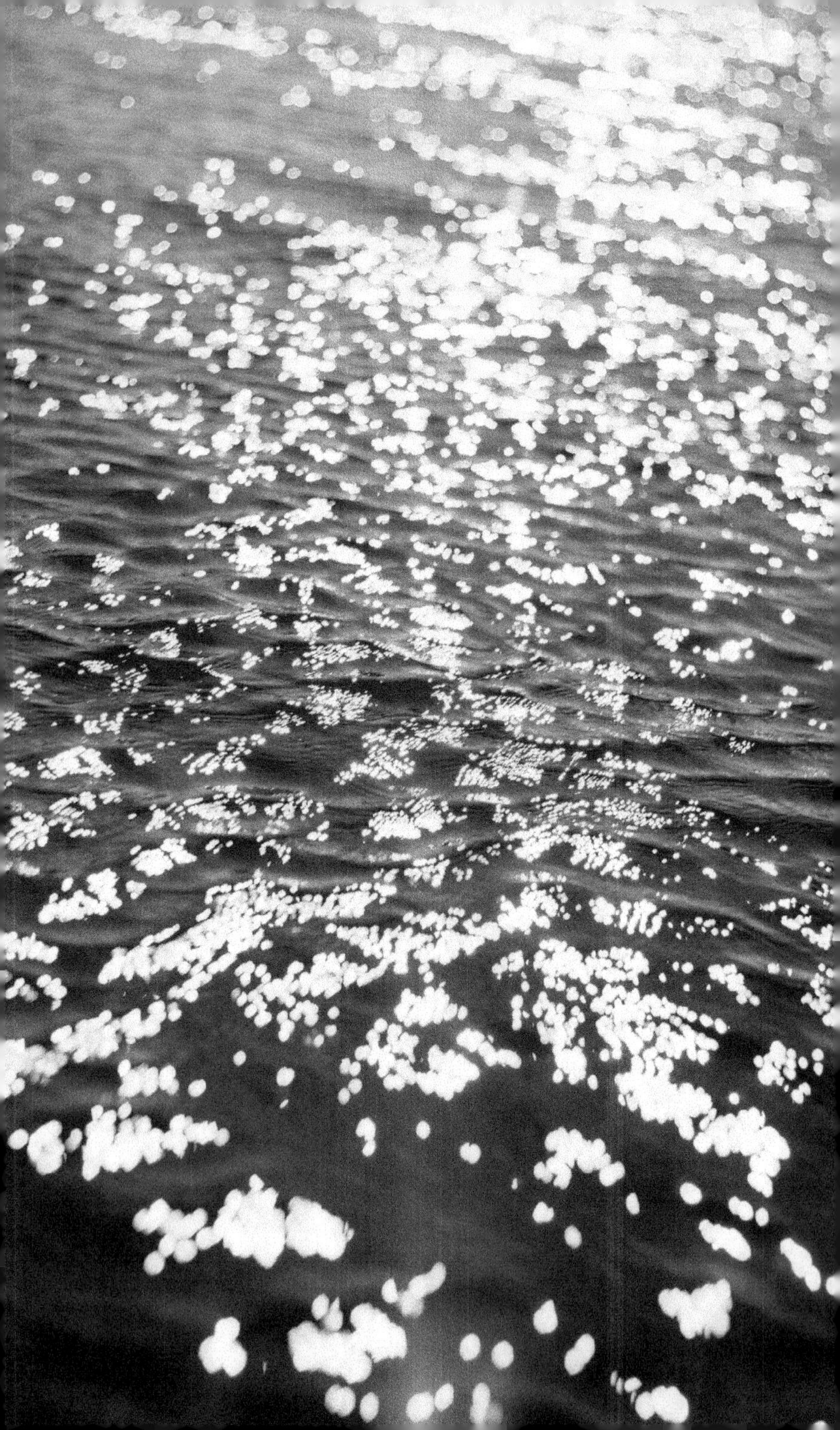

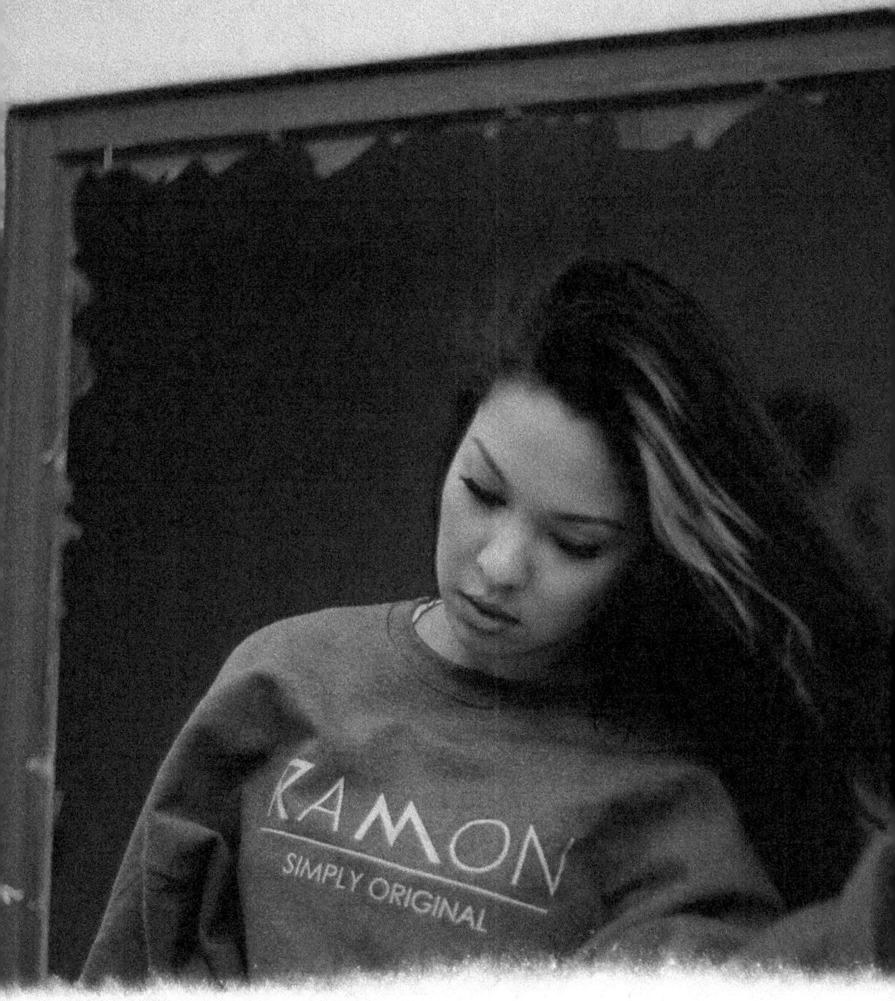
RAMON
SIMPLY ORIGINAL

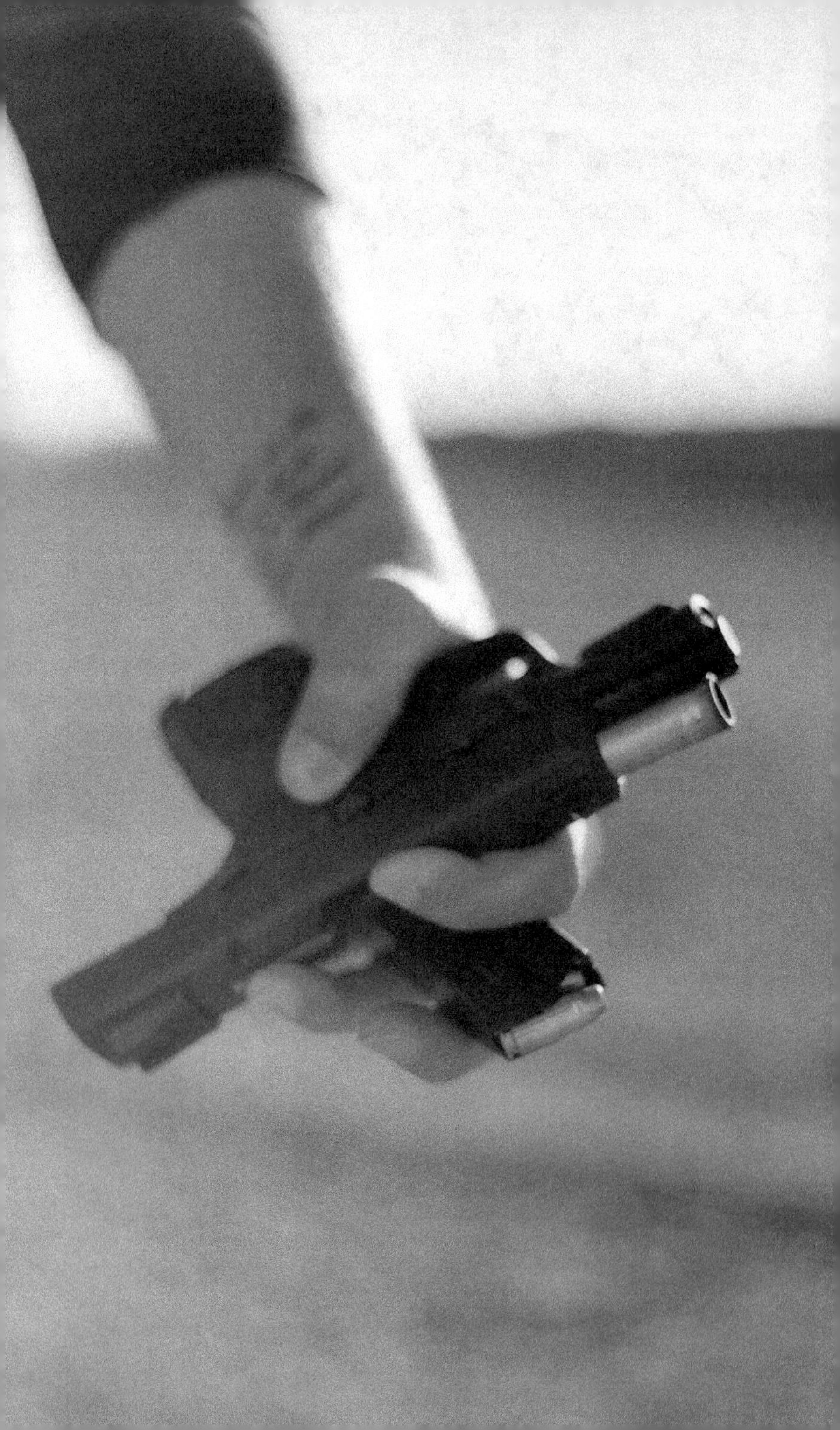

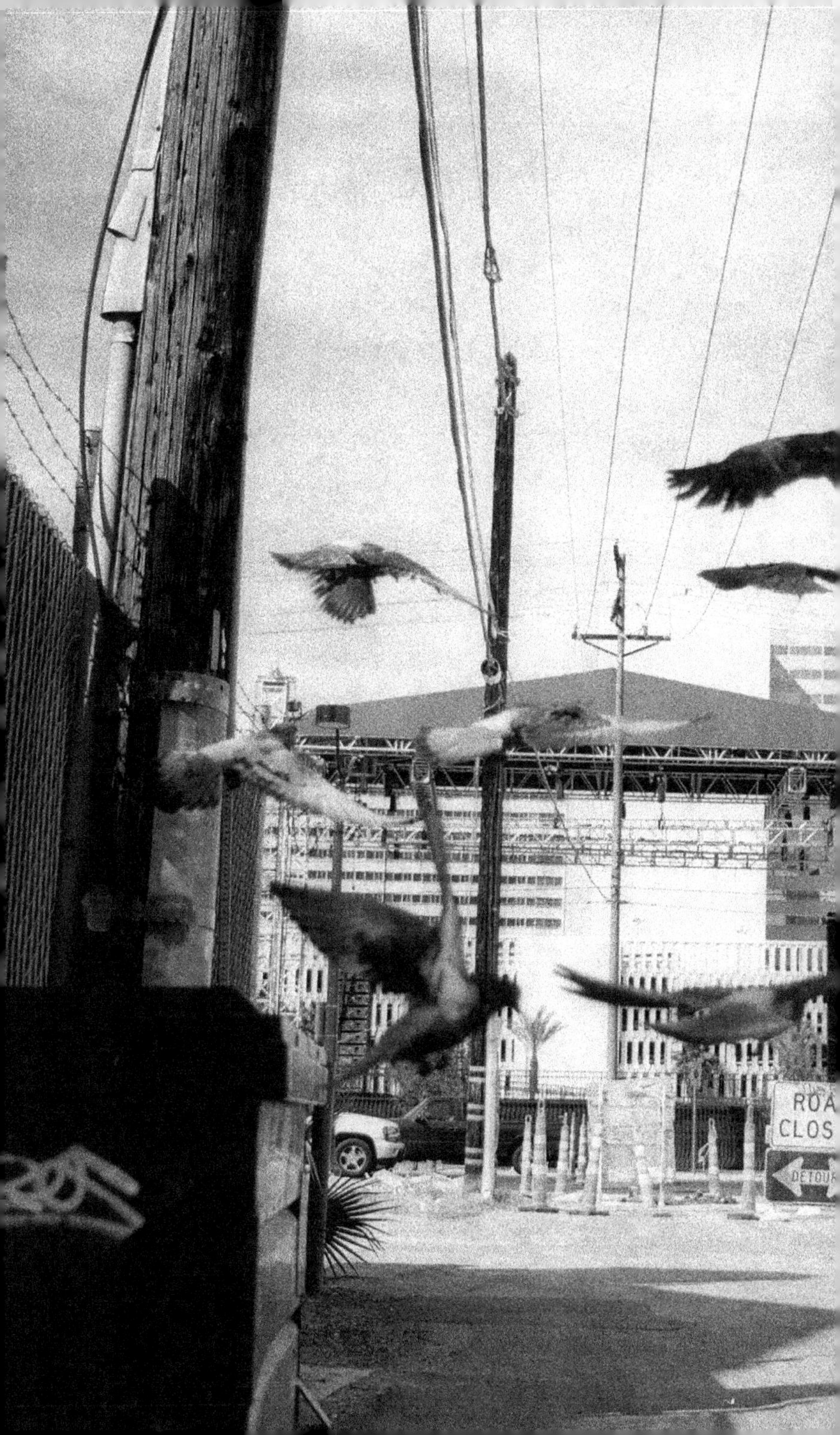
ROA
CLOS

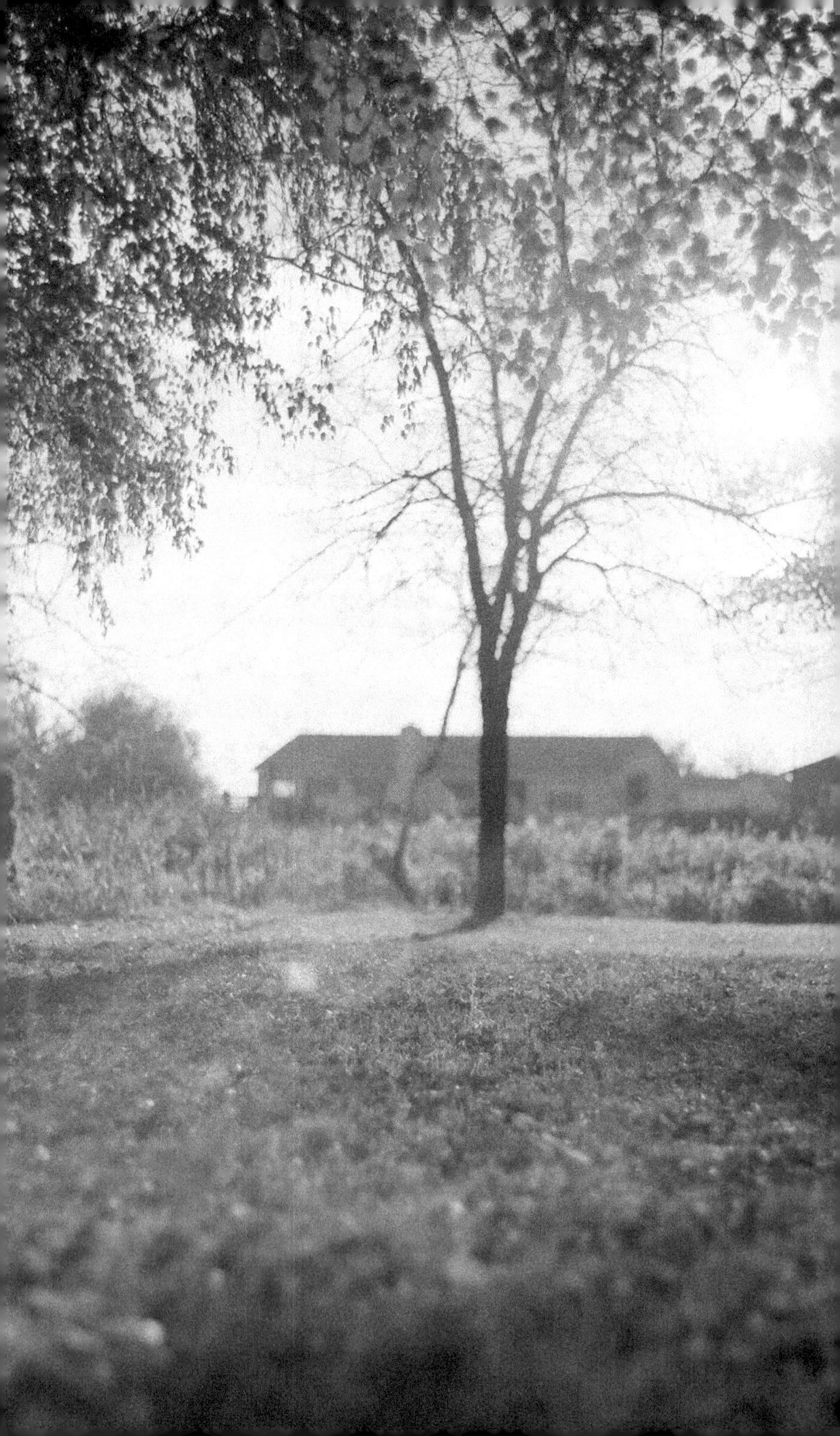

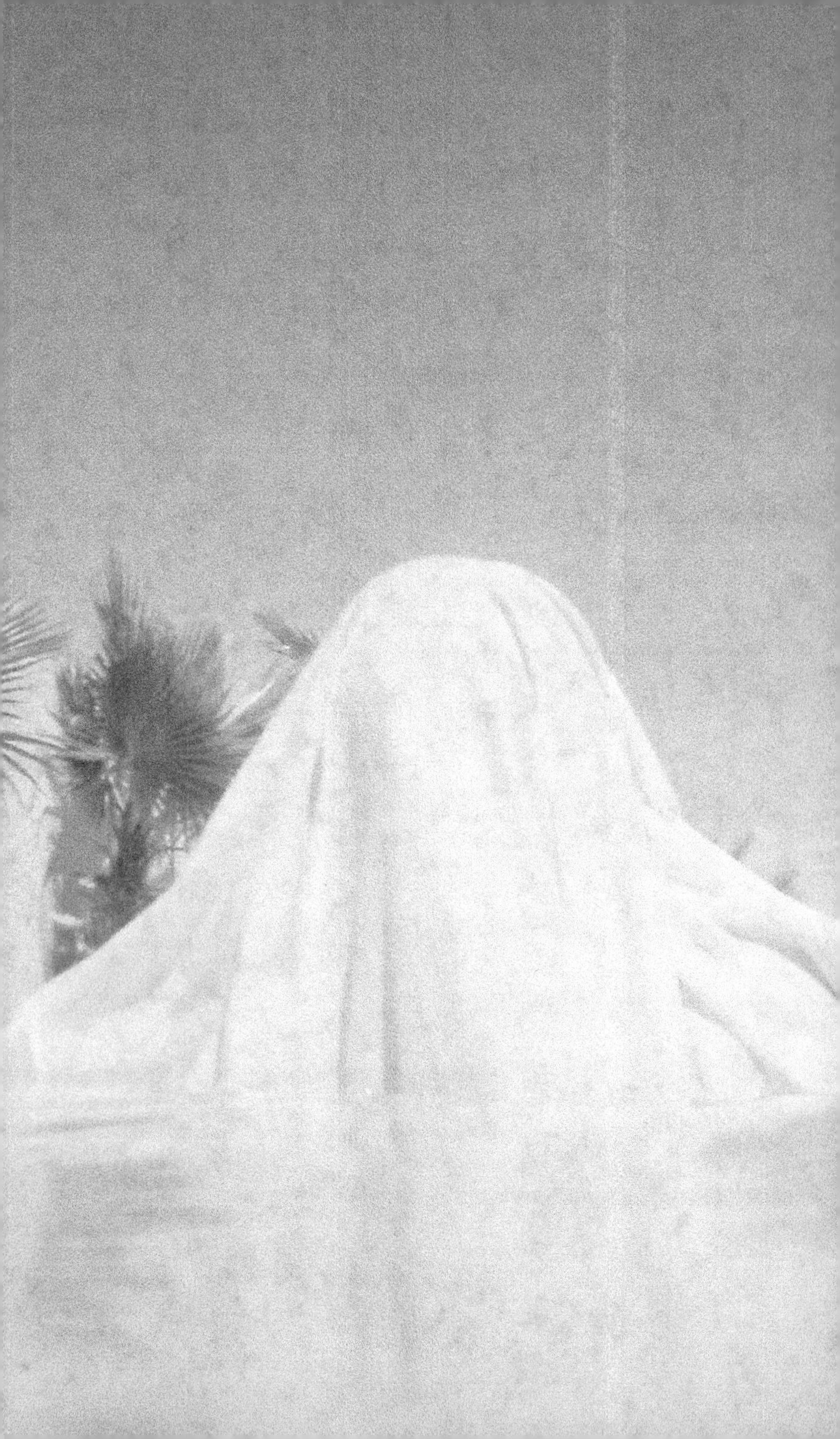

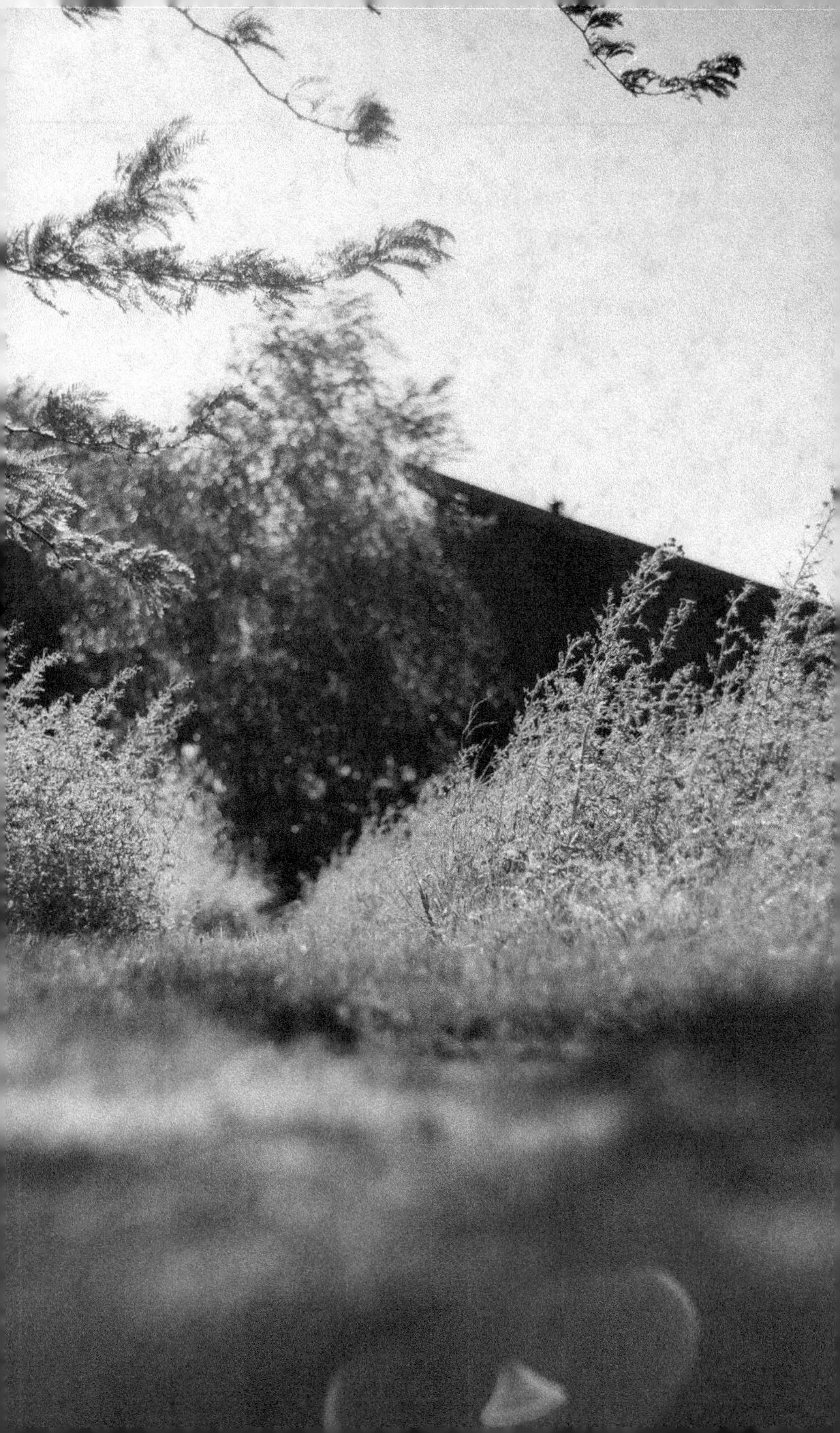

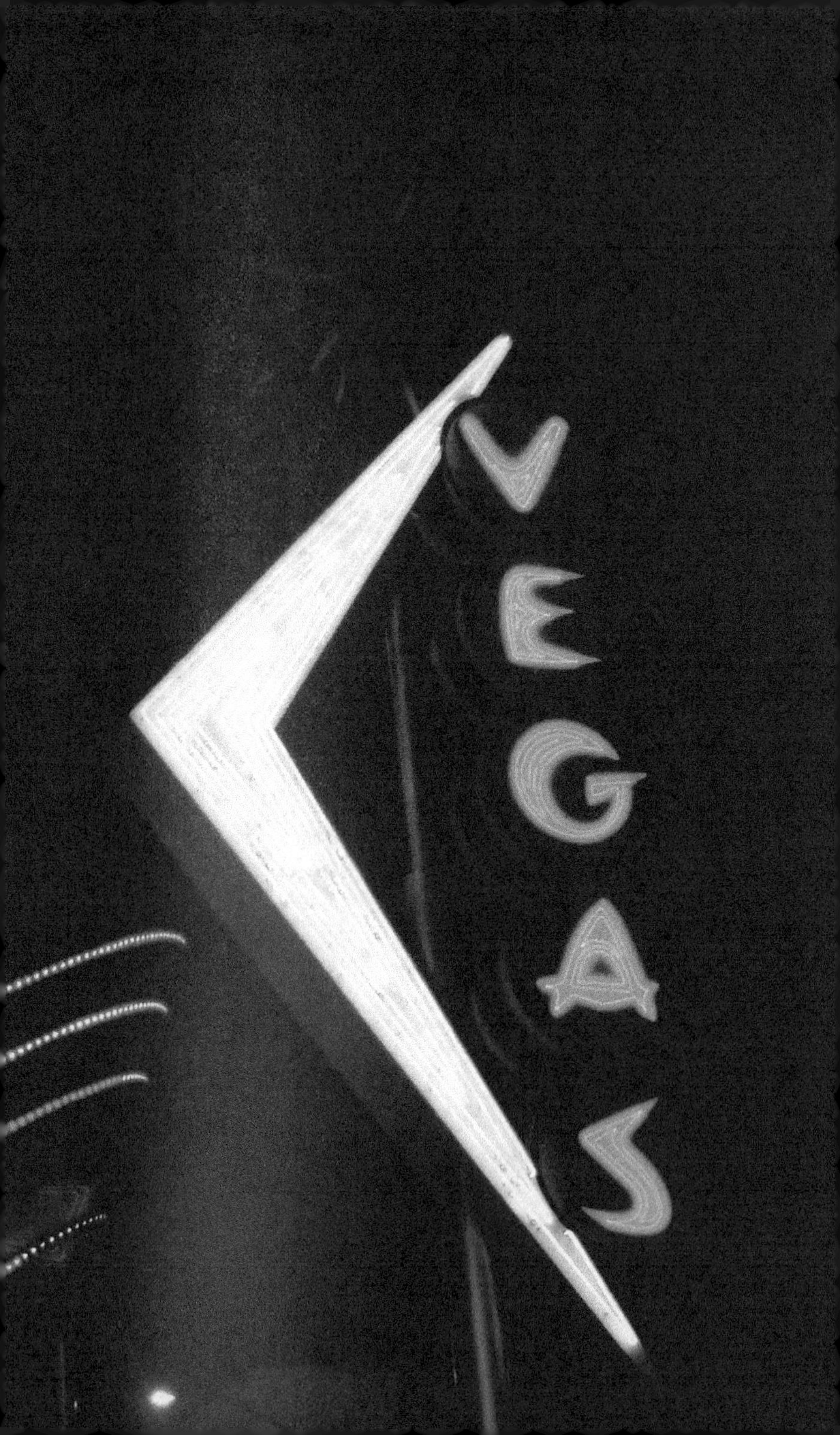
VEGAS

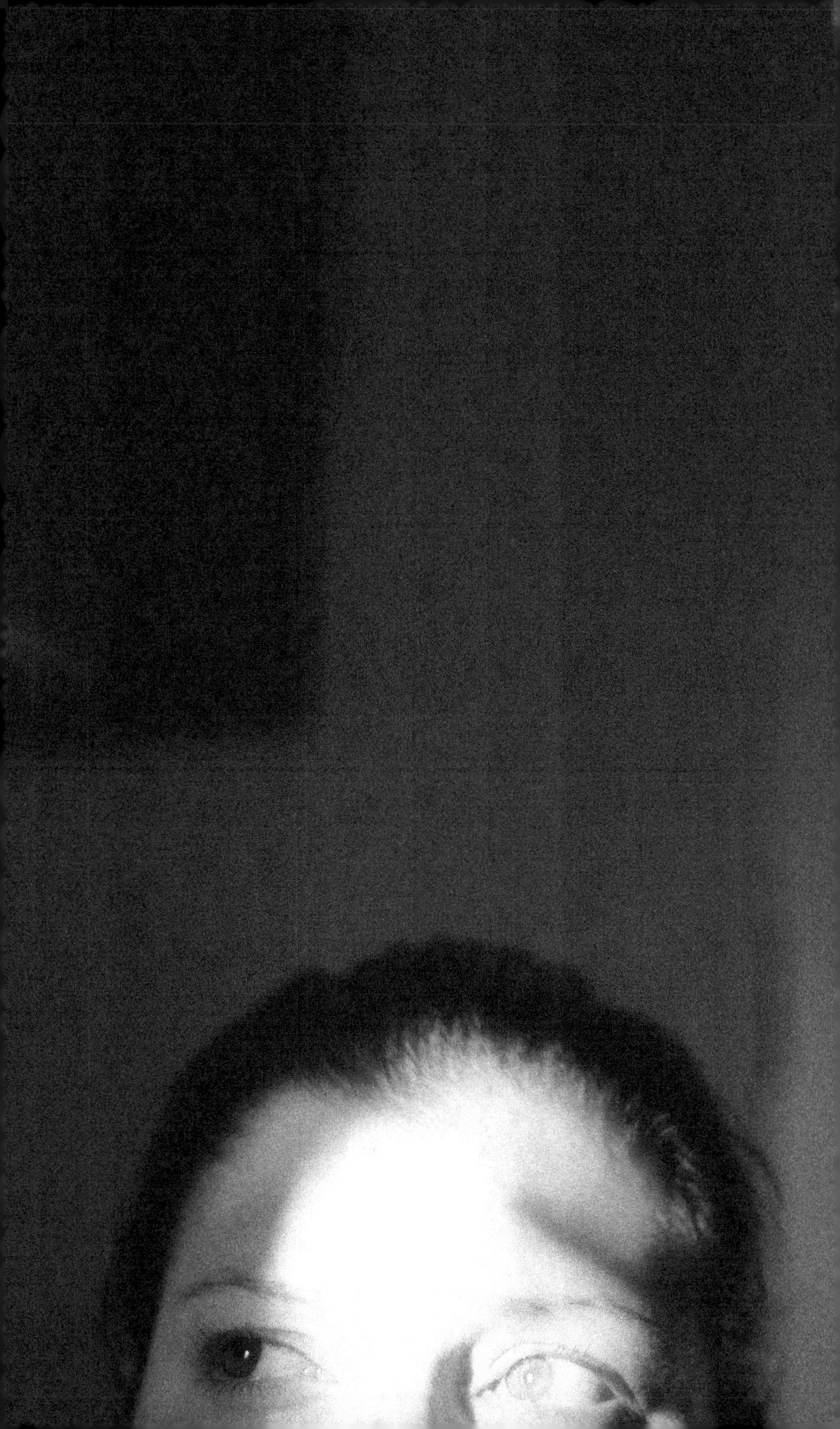

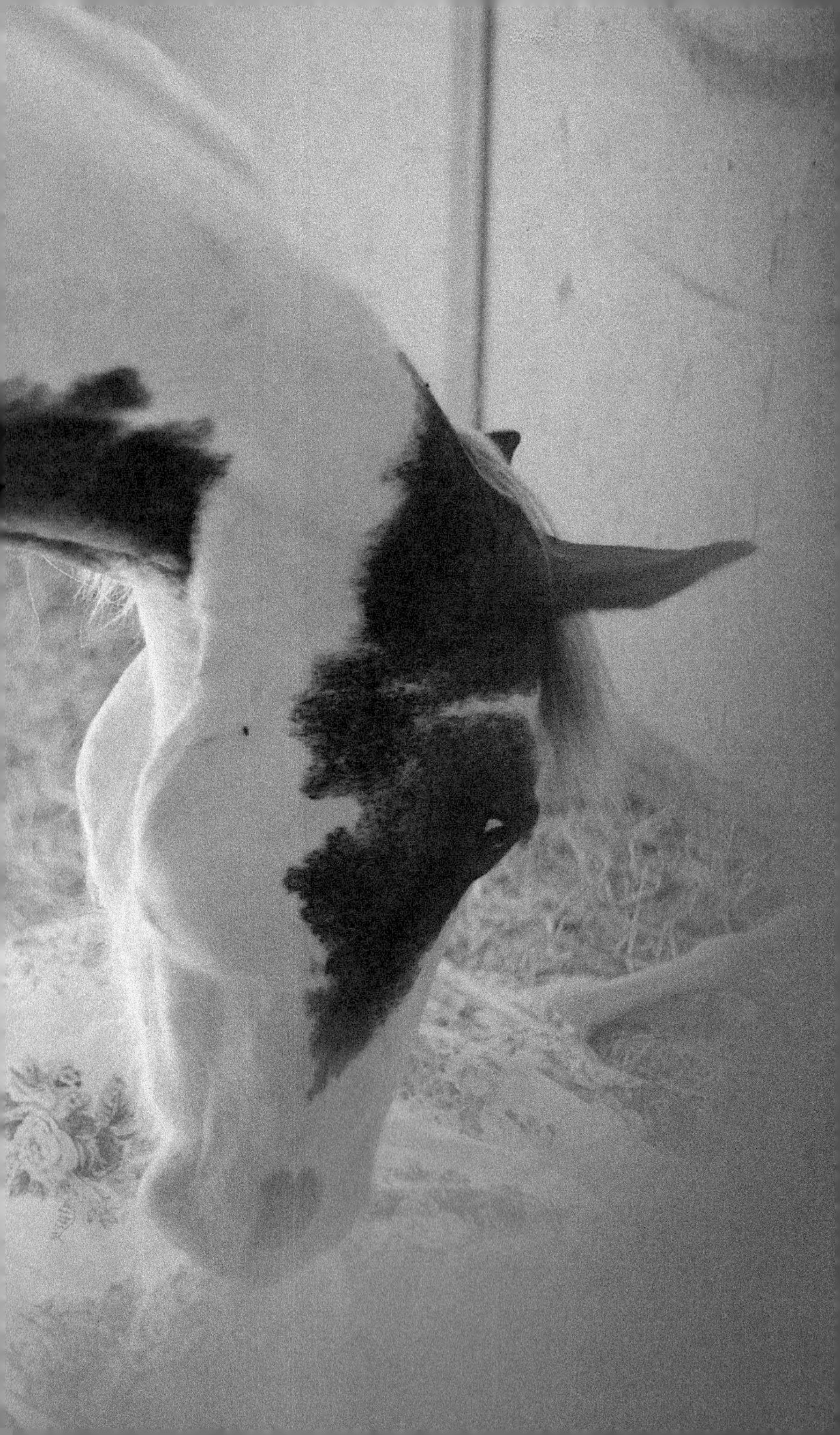

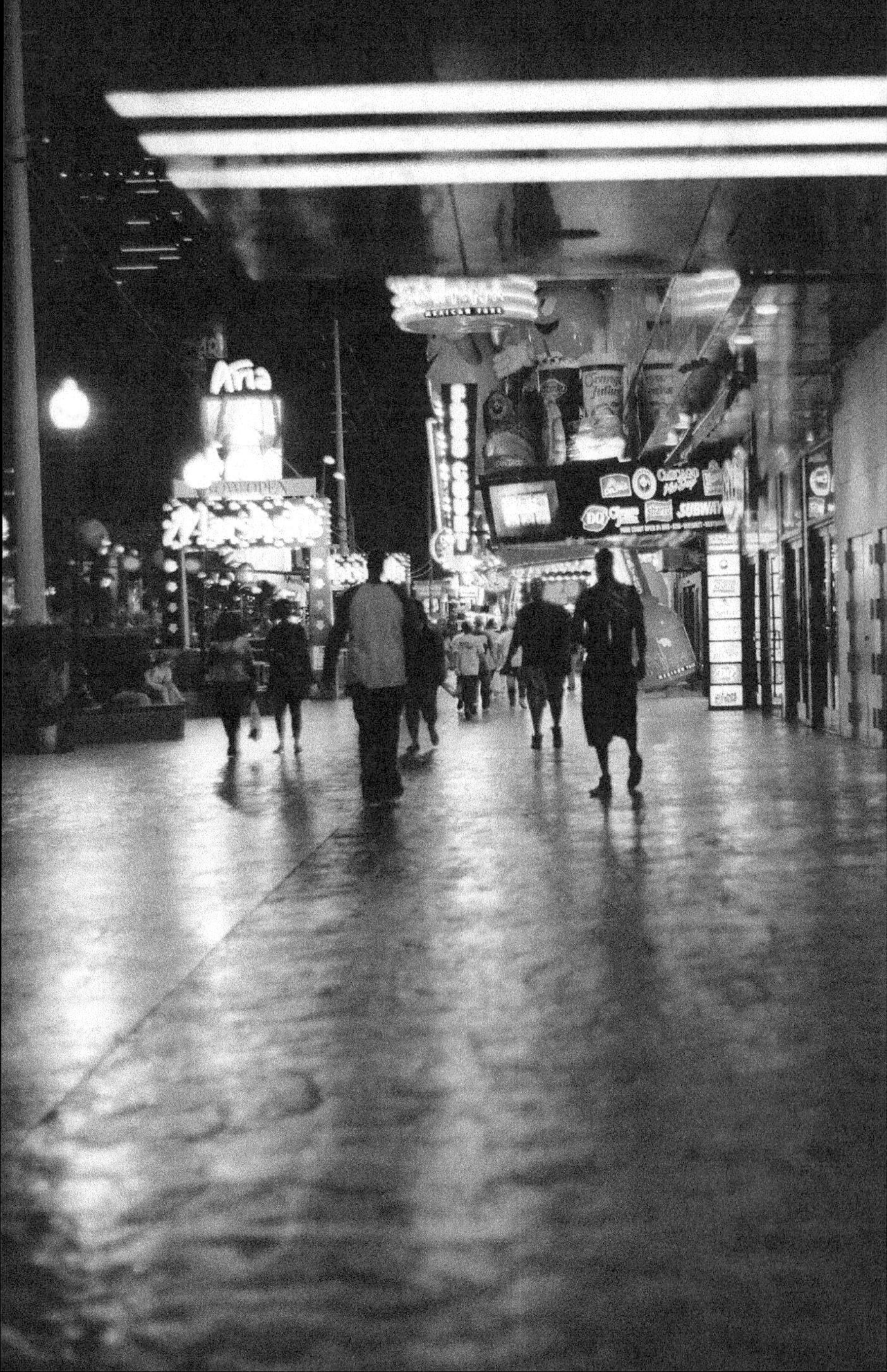
Aria
SUBWAY

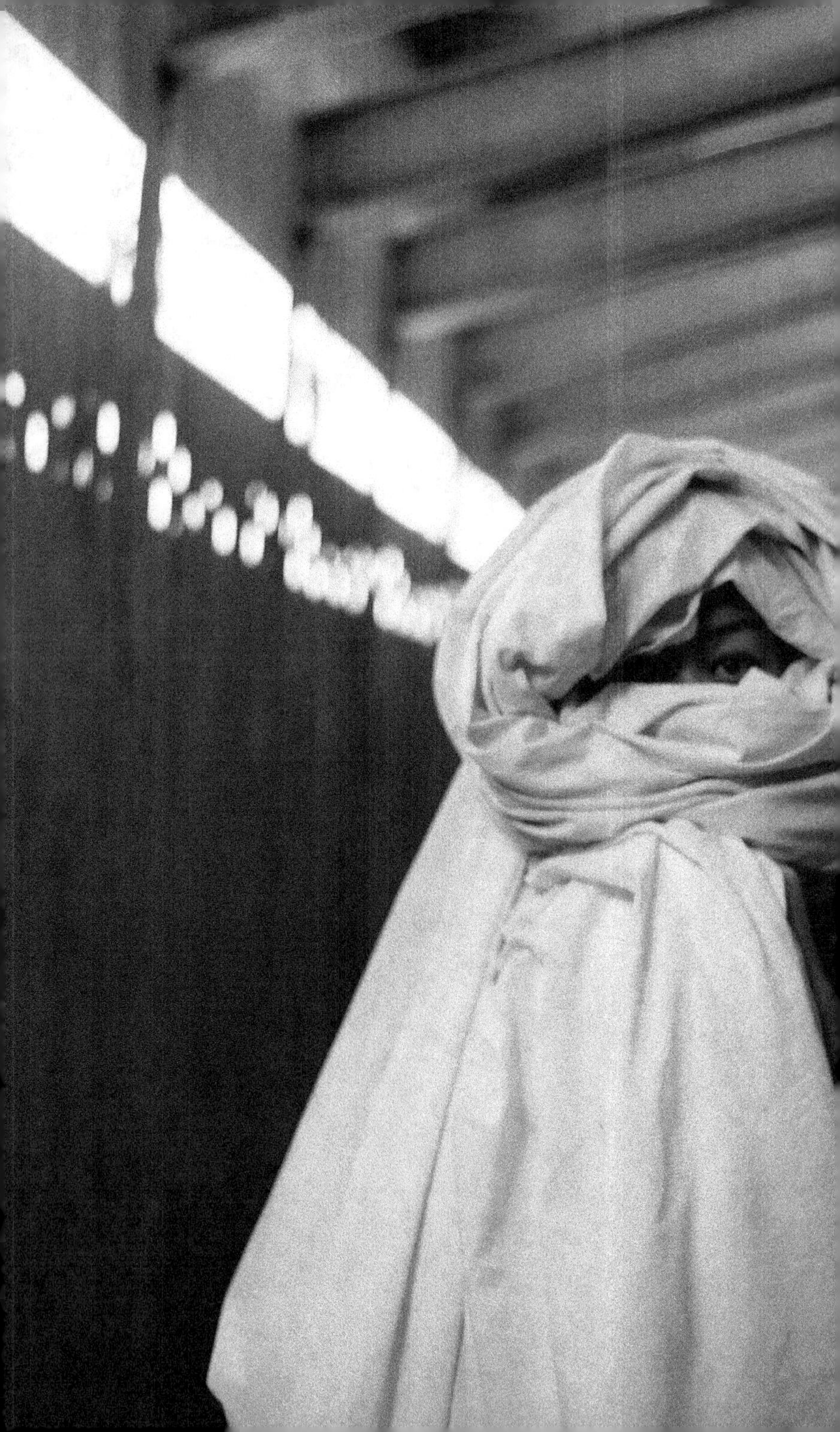

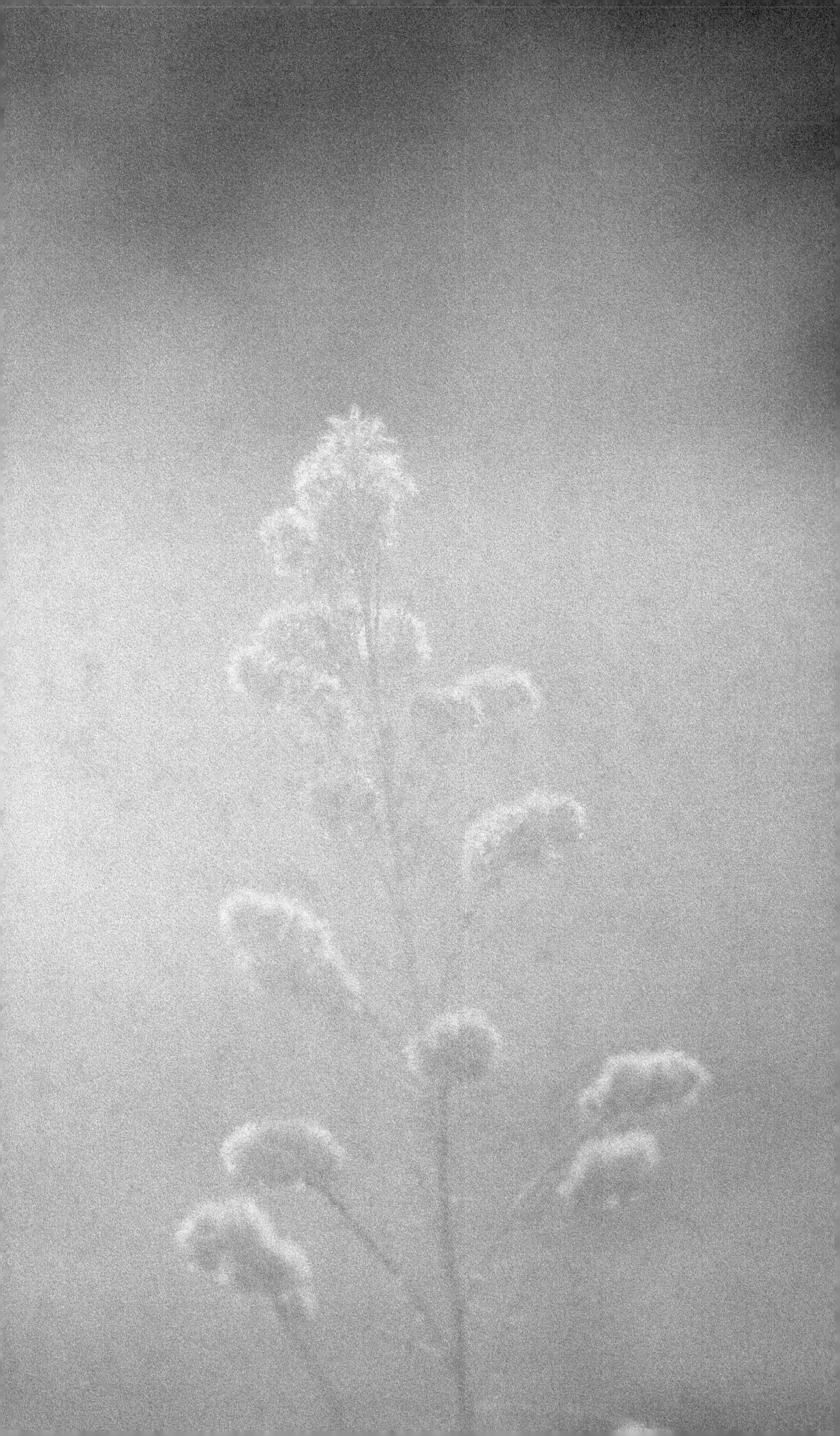

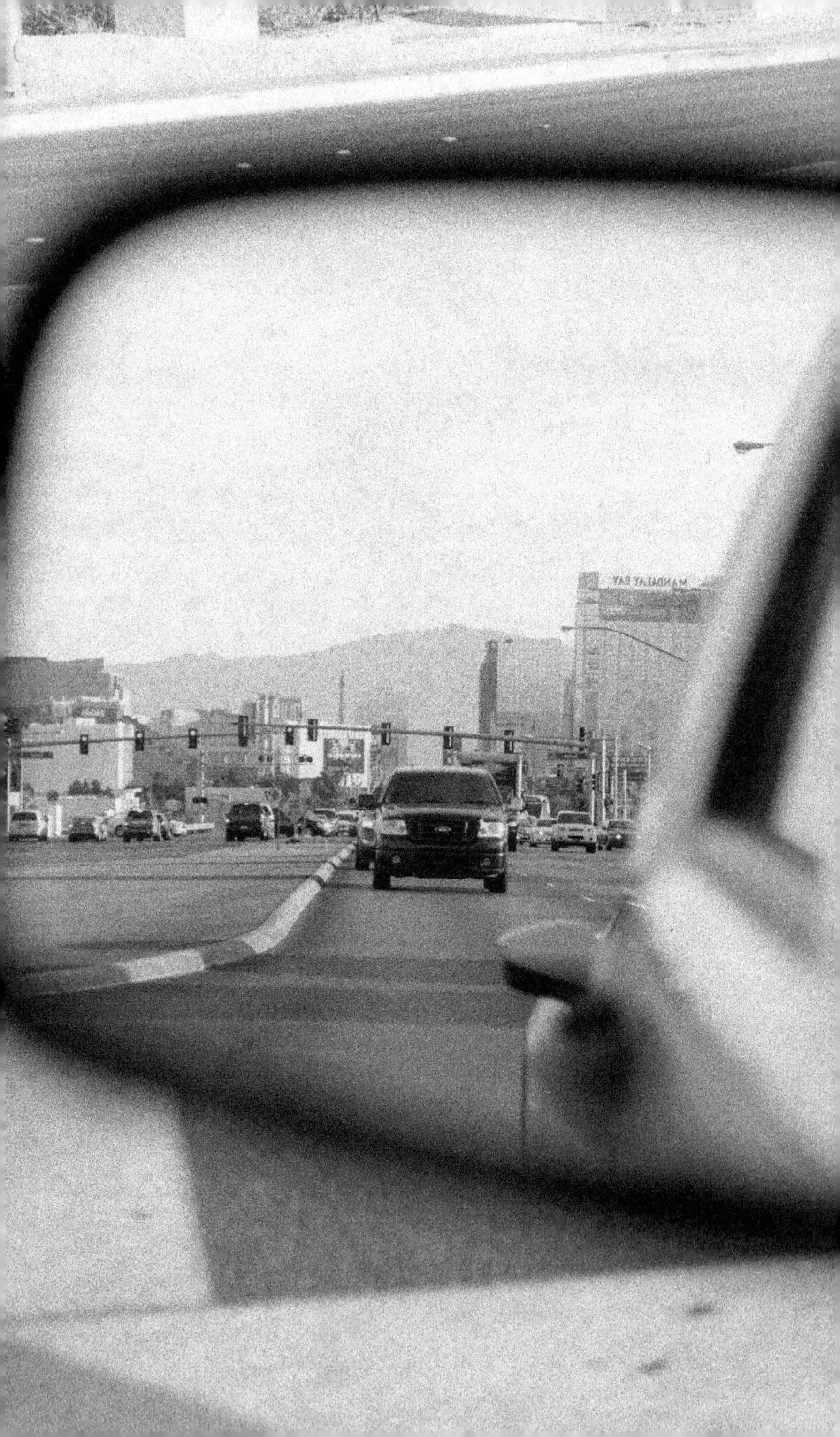

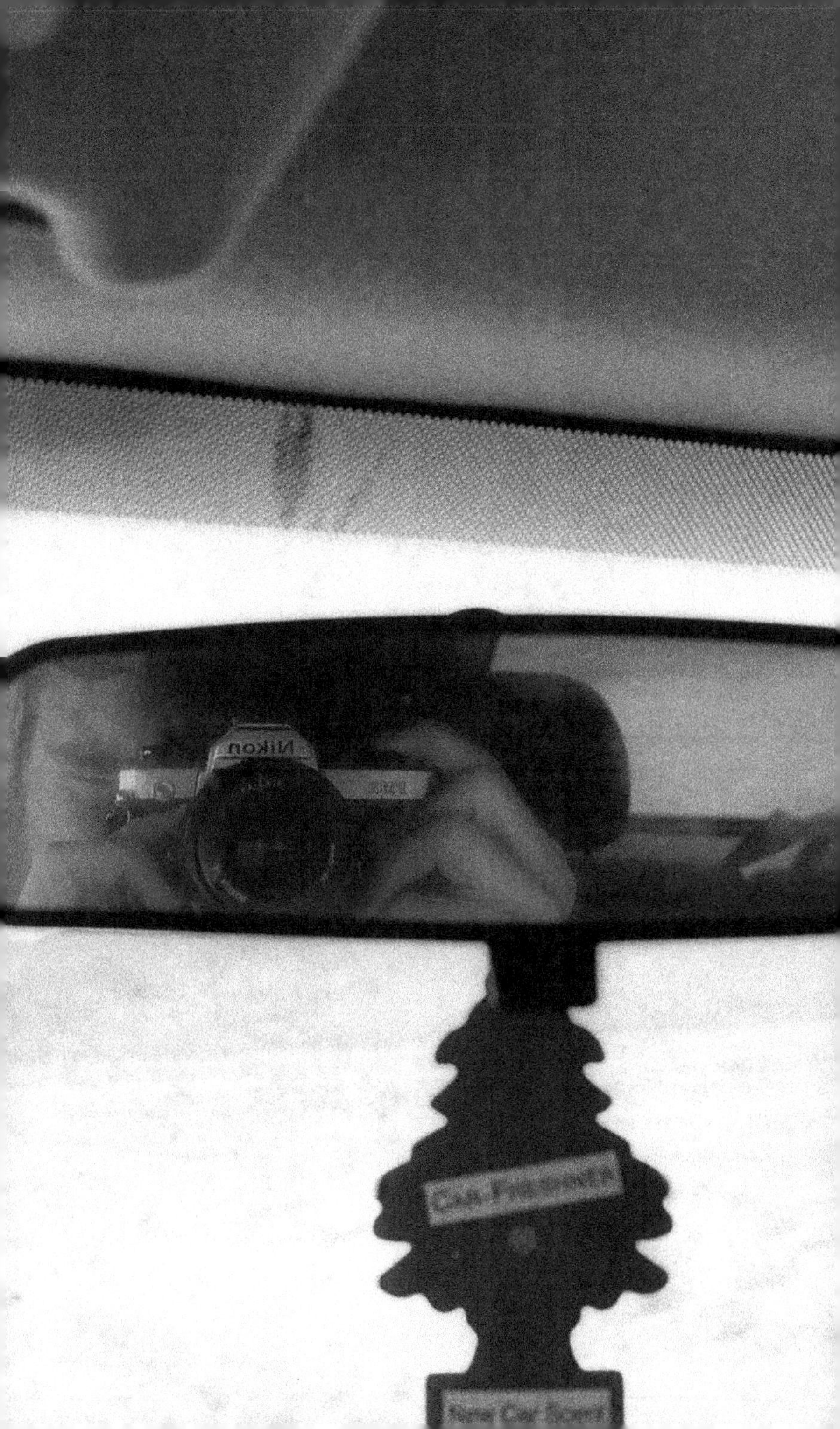
Nikon

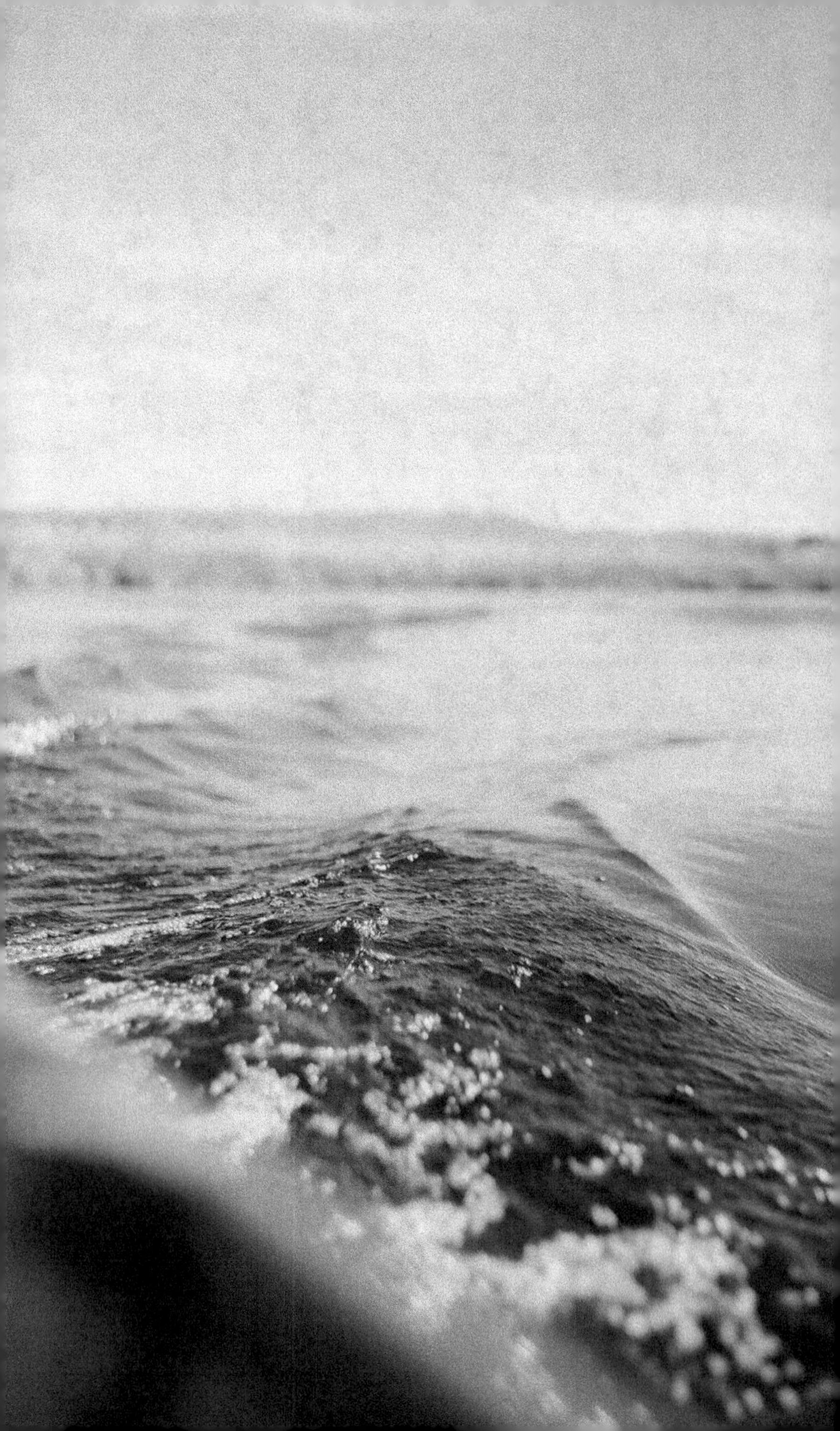

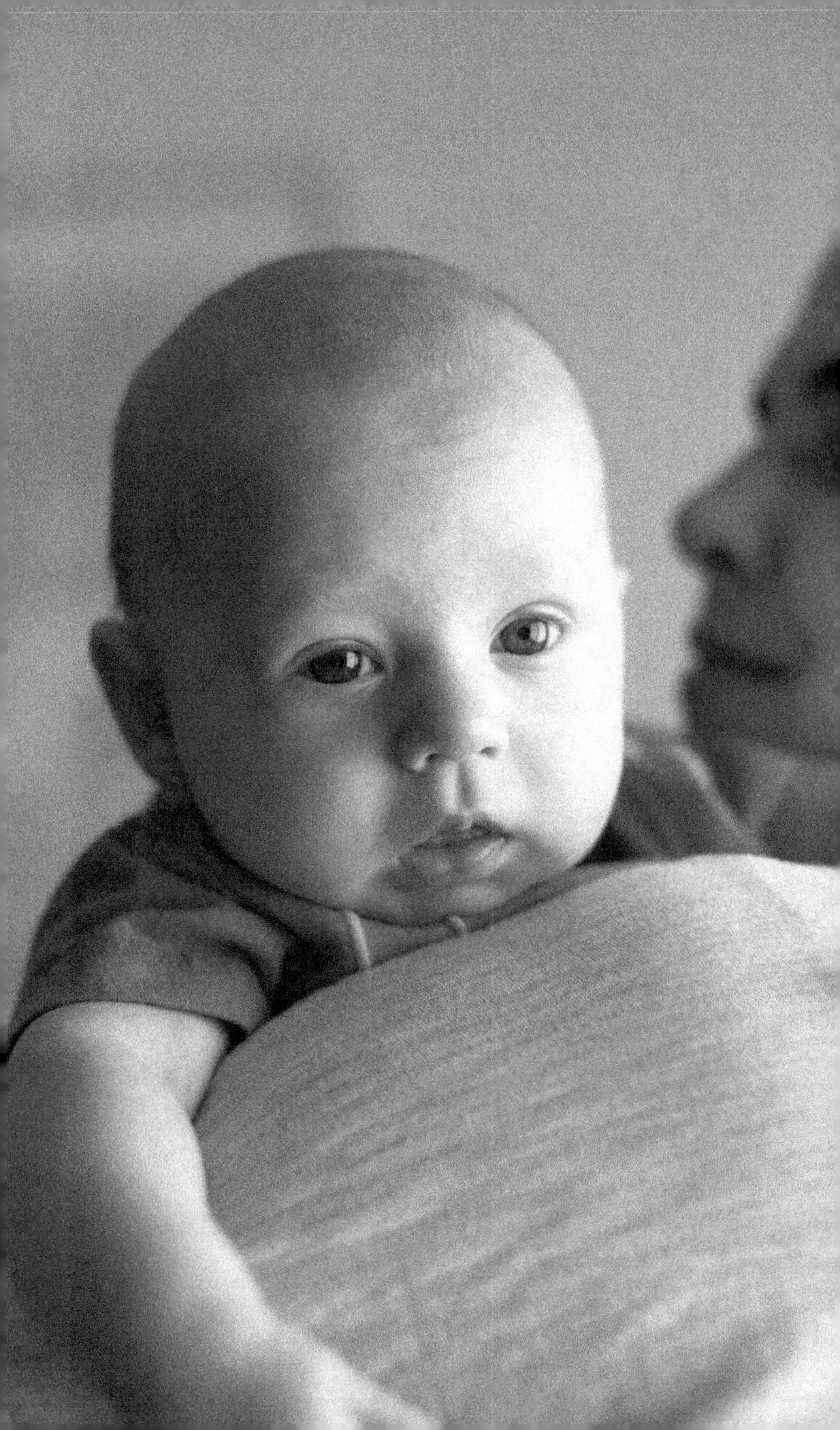

Monte Carlo
NEW YORK
NEW YORK
MANDALAY BAY

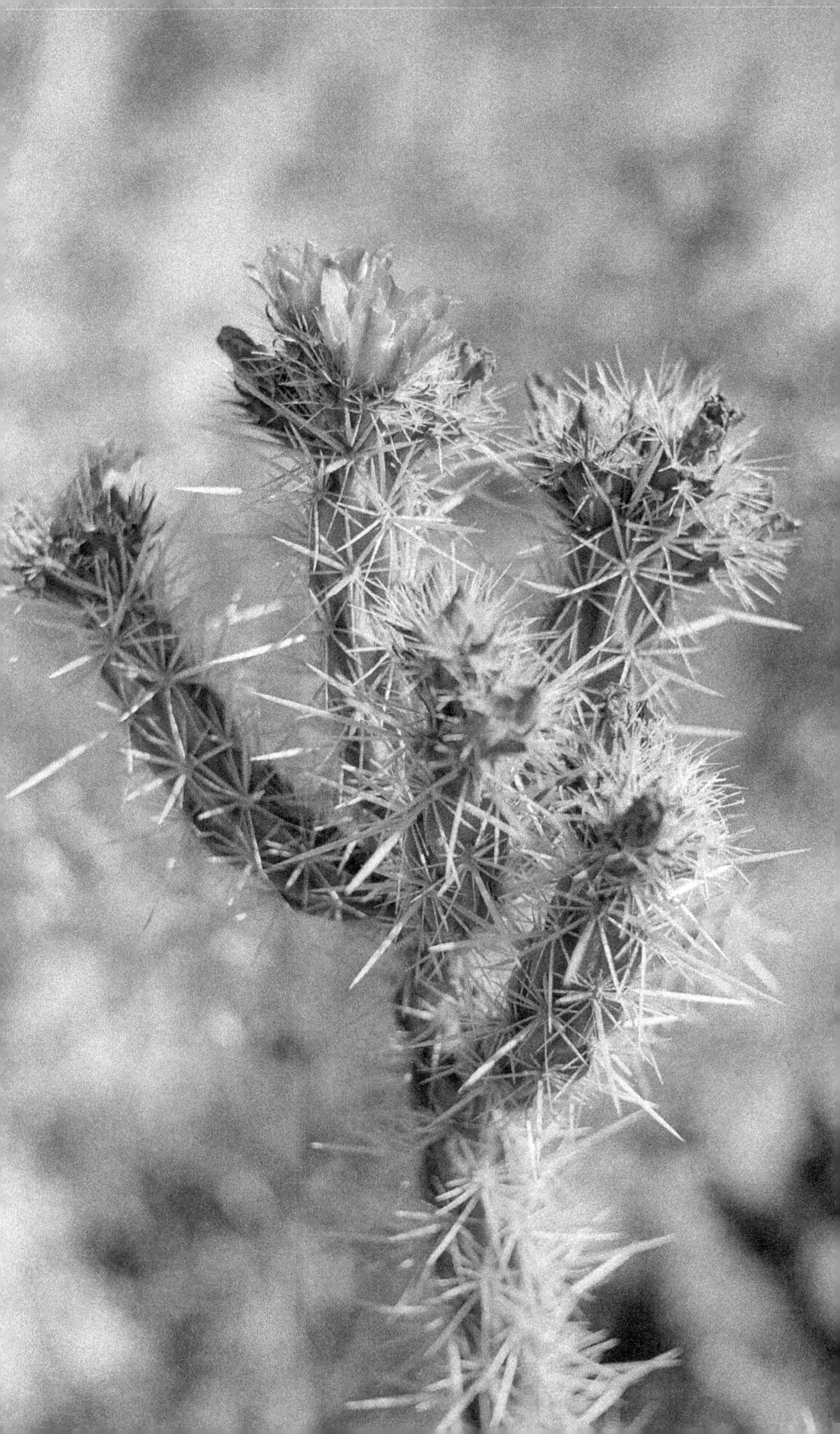

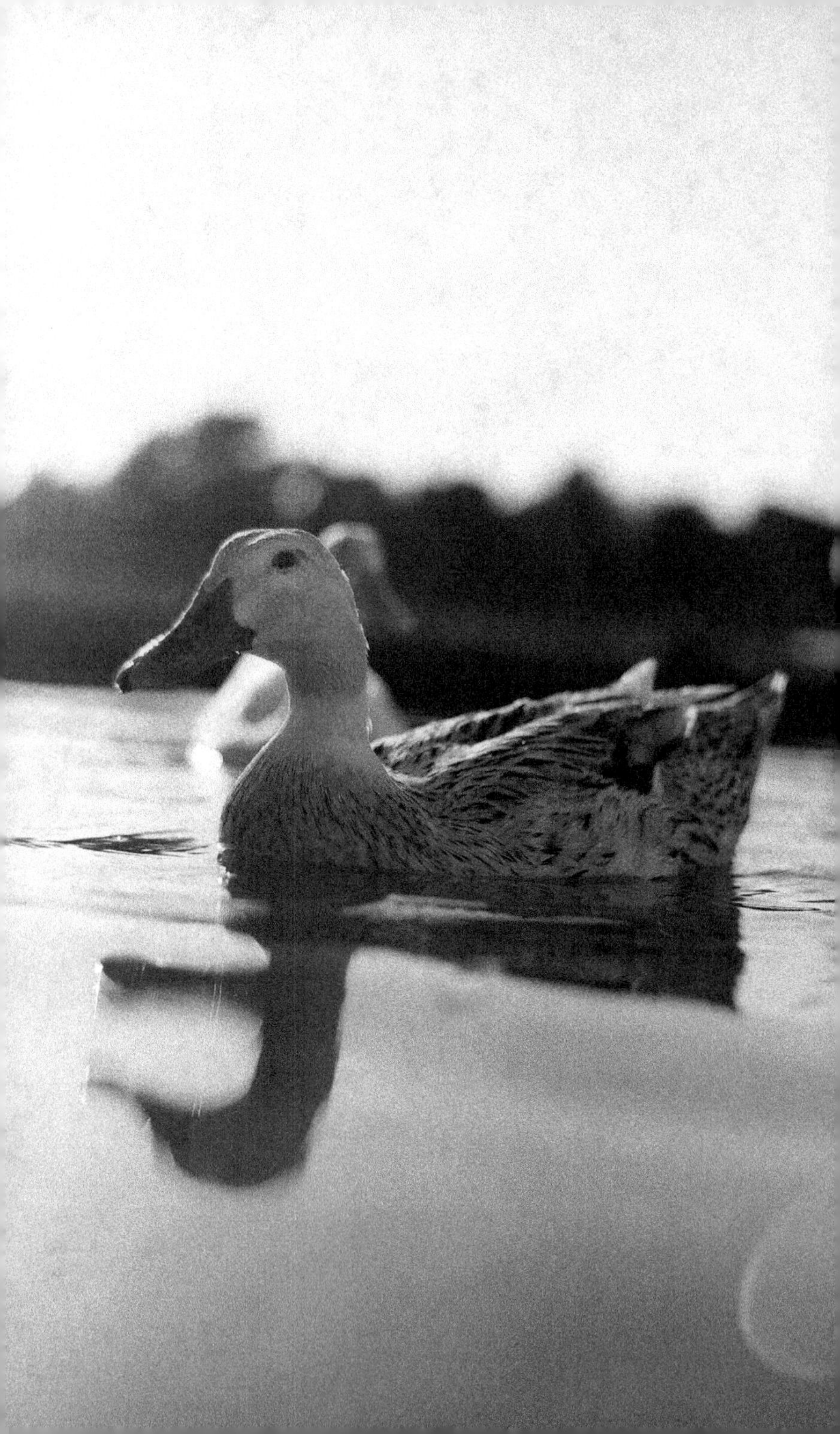

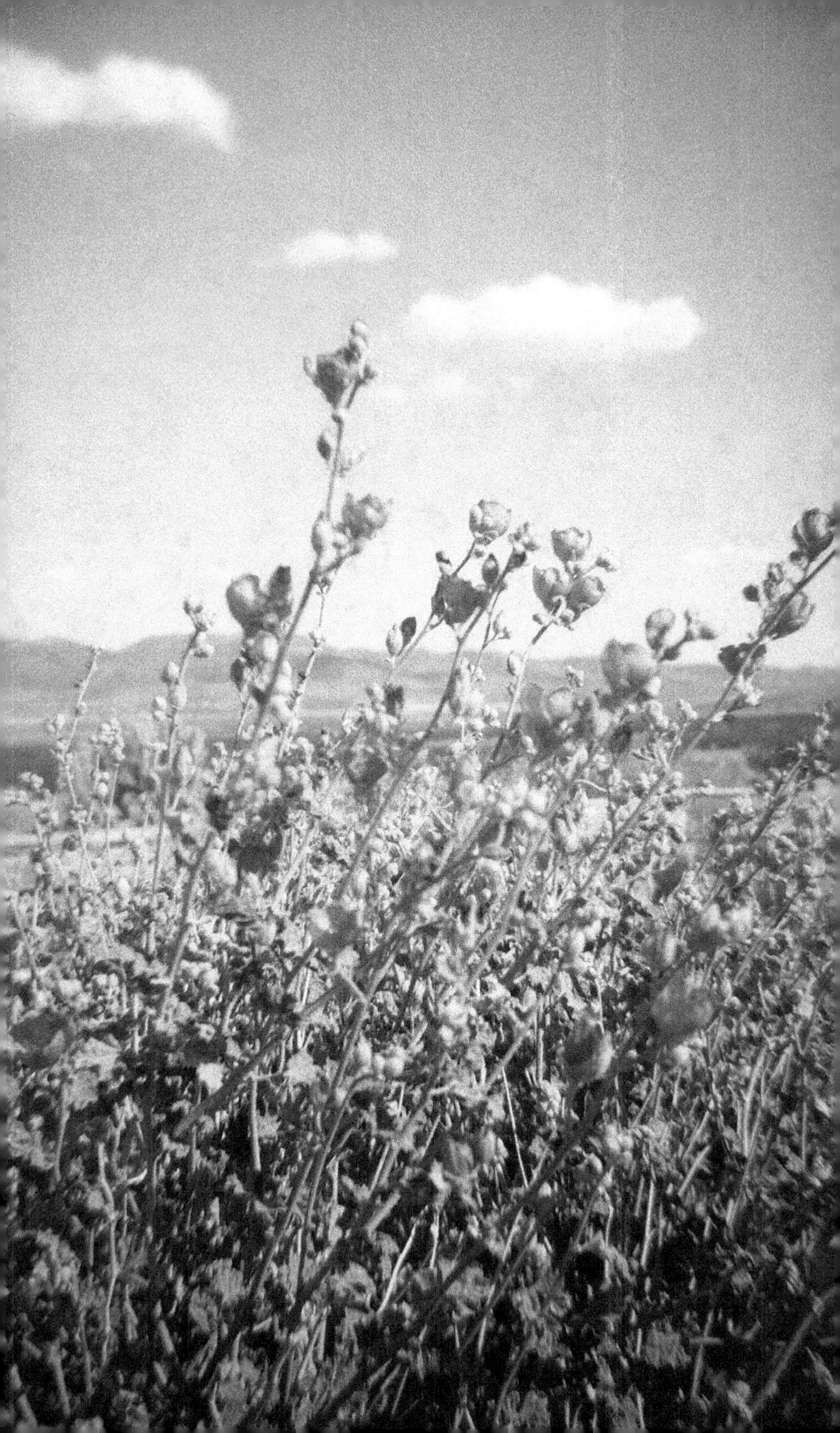

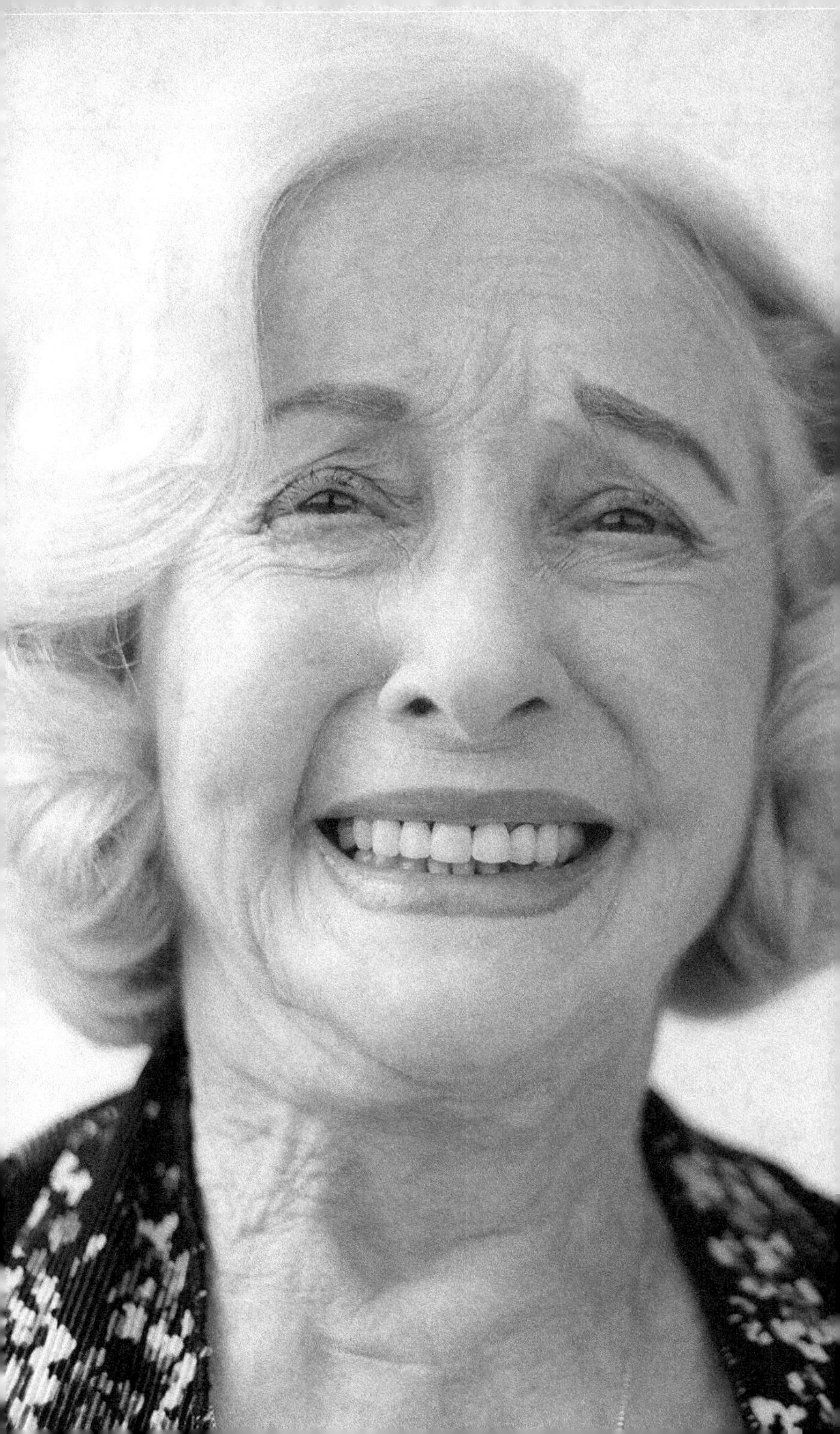

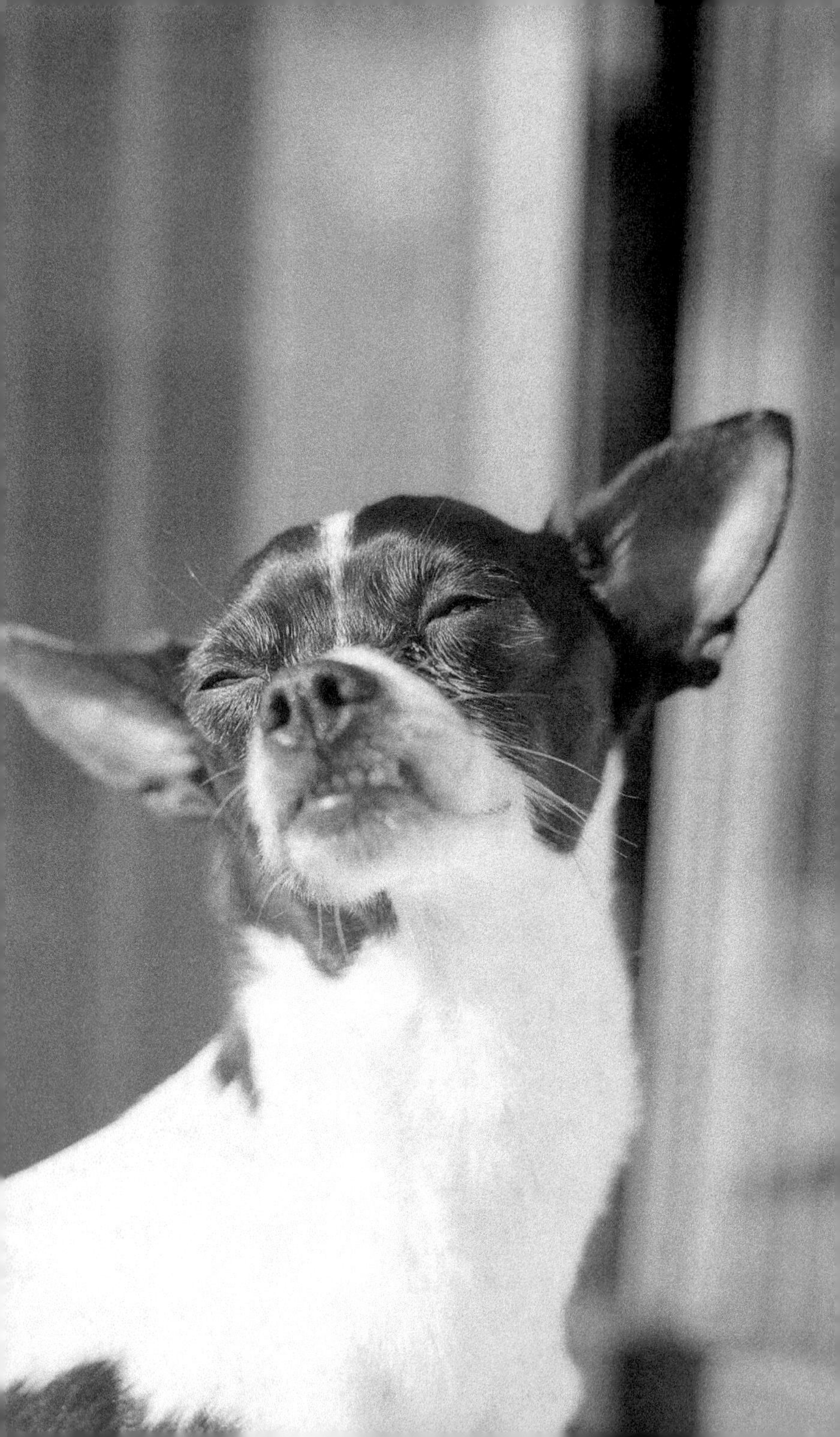

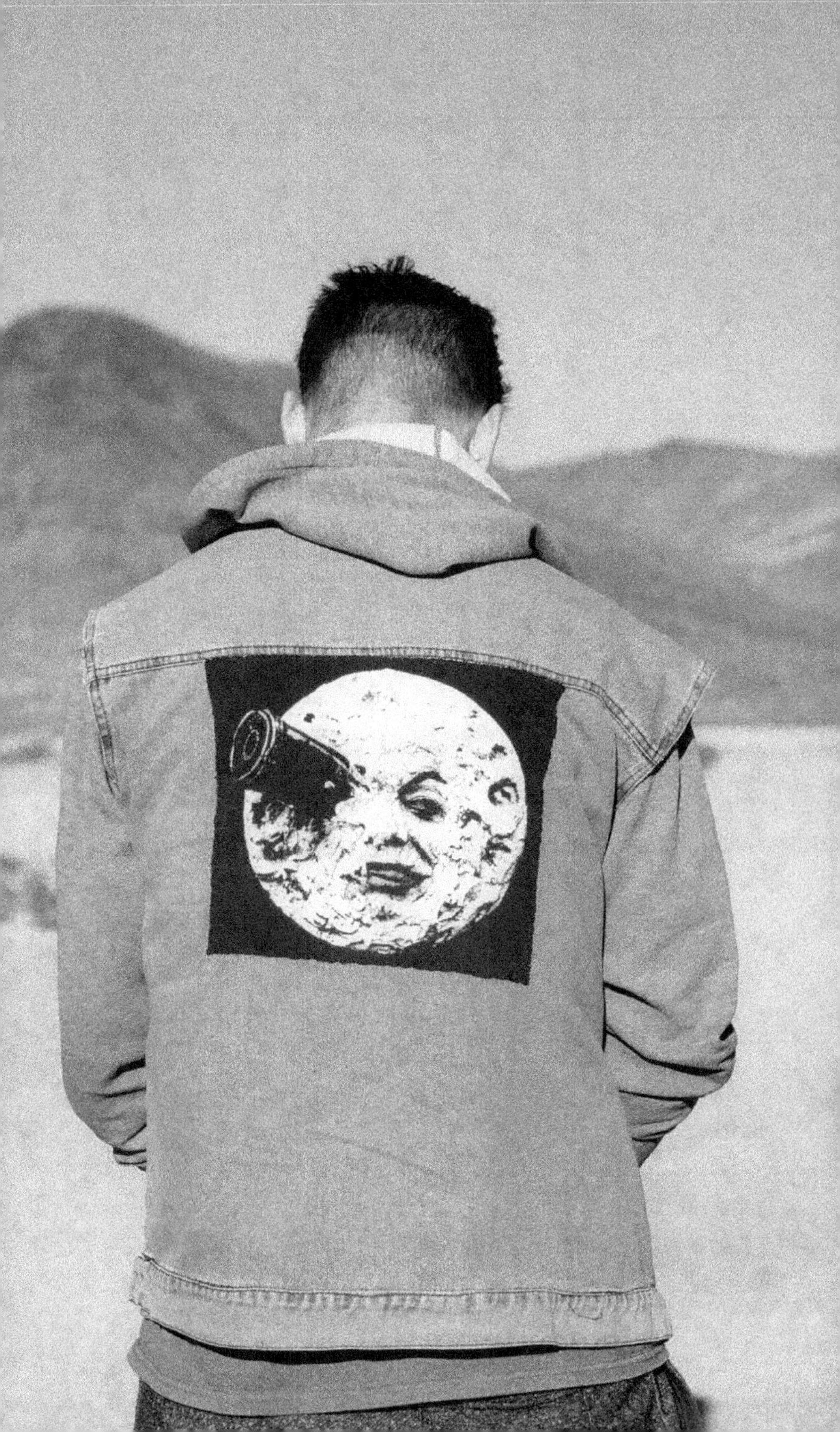

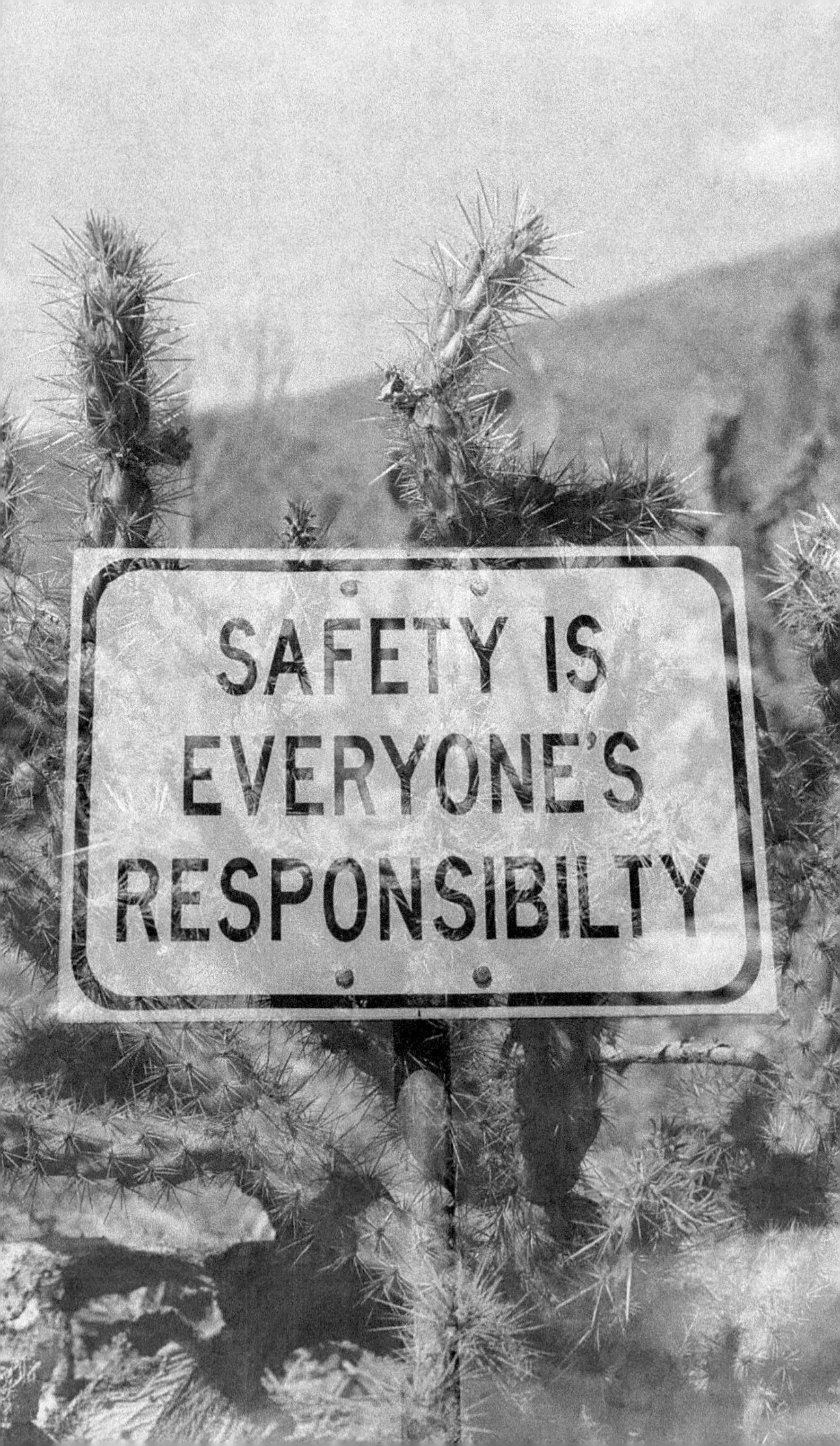
SAFETY IS
EVERYONE'S
RESPONSIBILTY

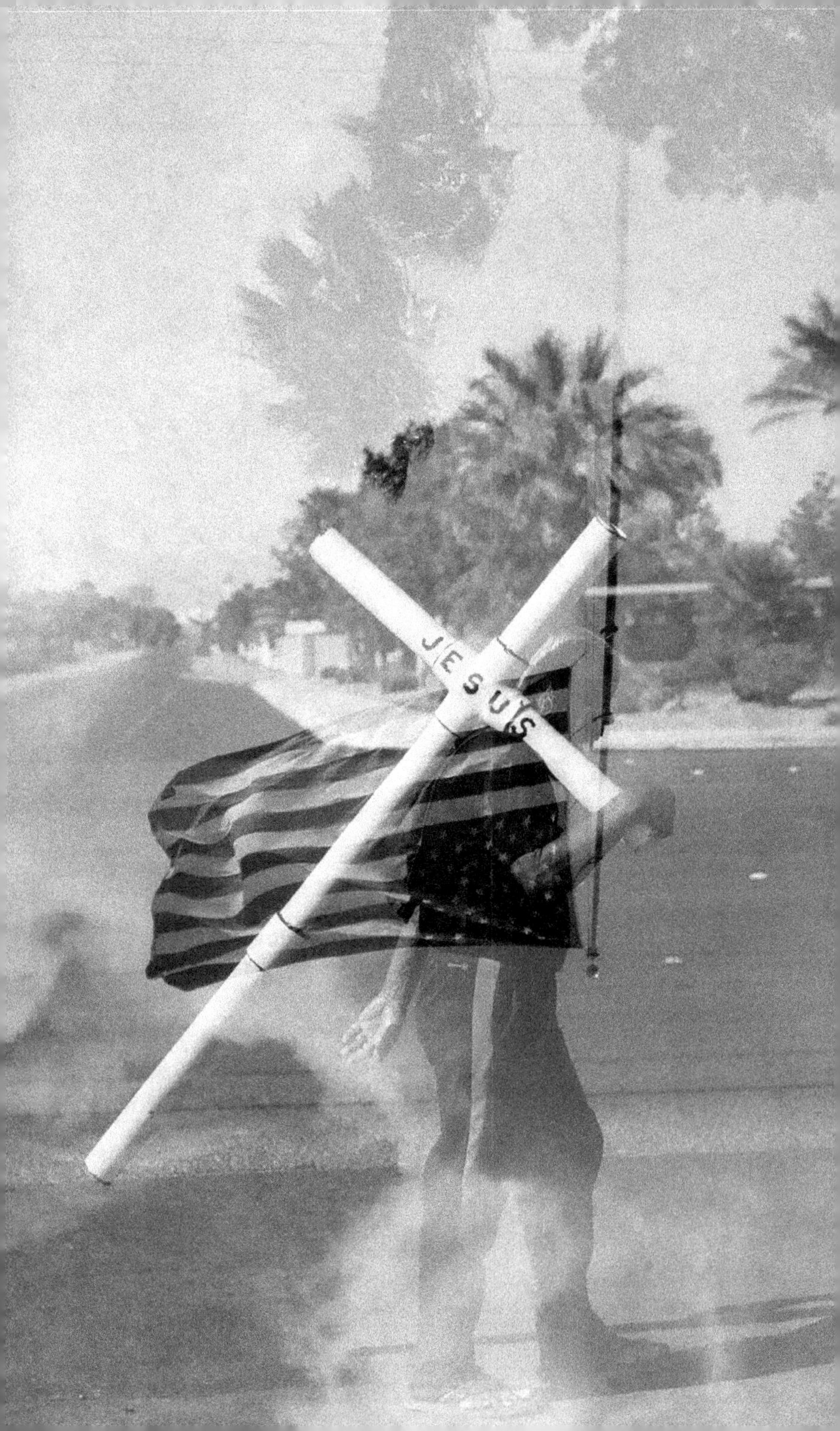
JESUS

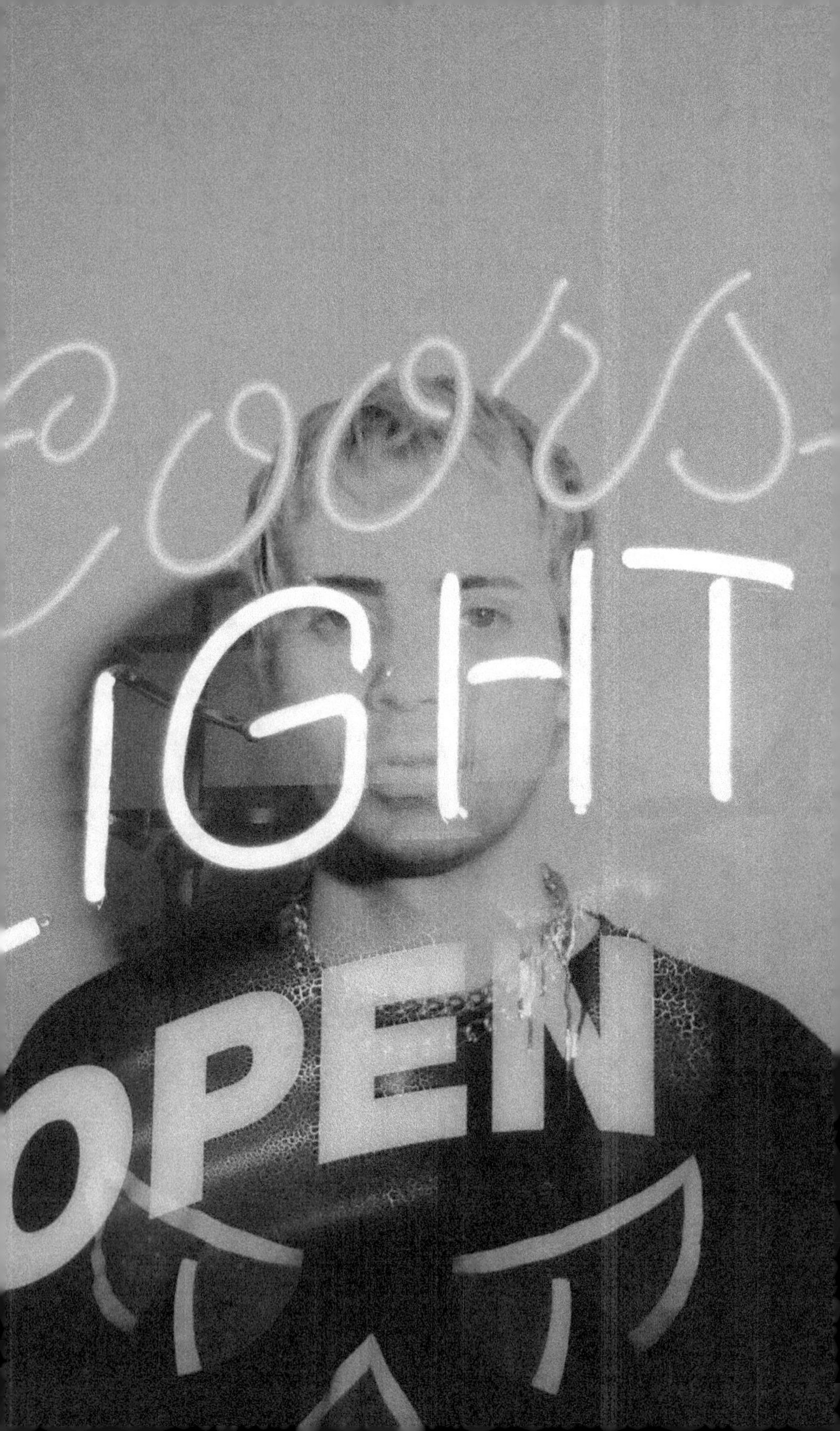
IGHT
OPEN

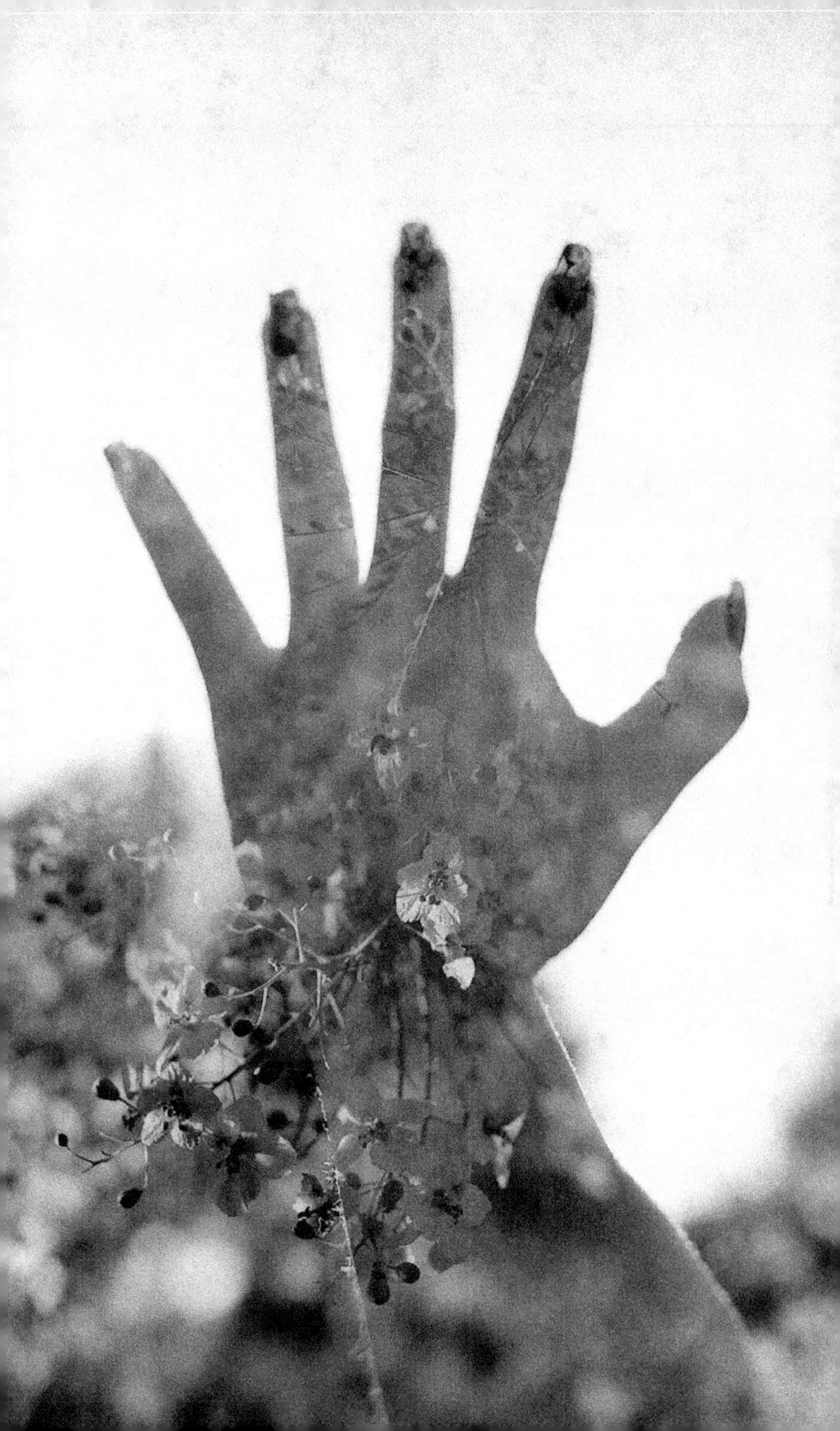

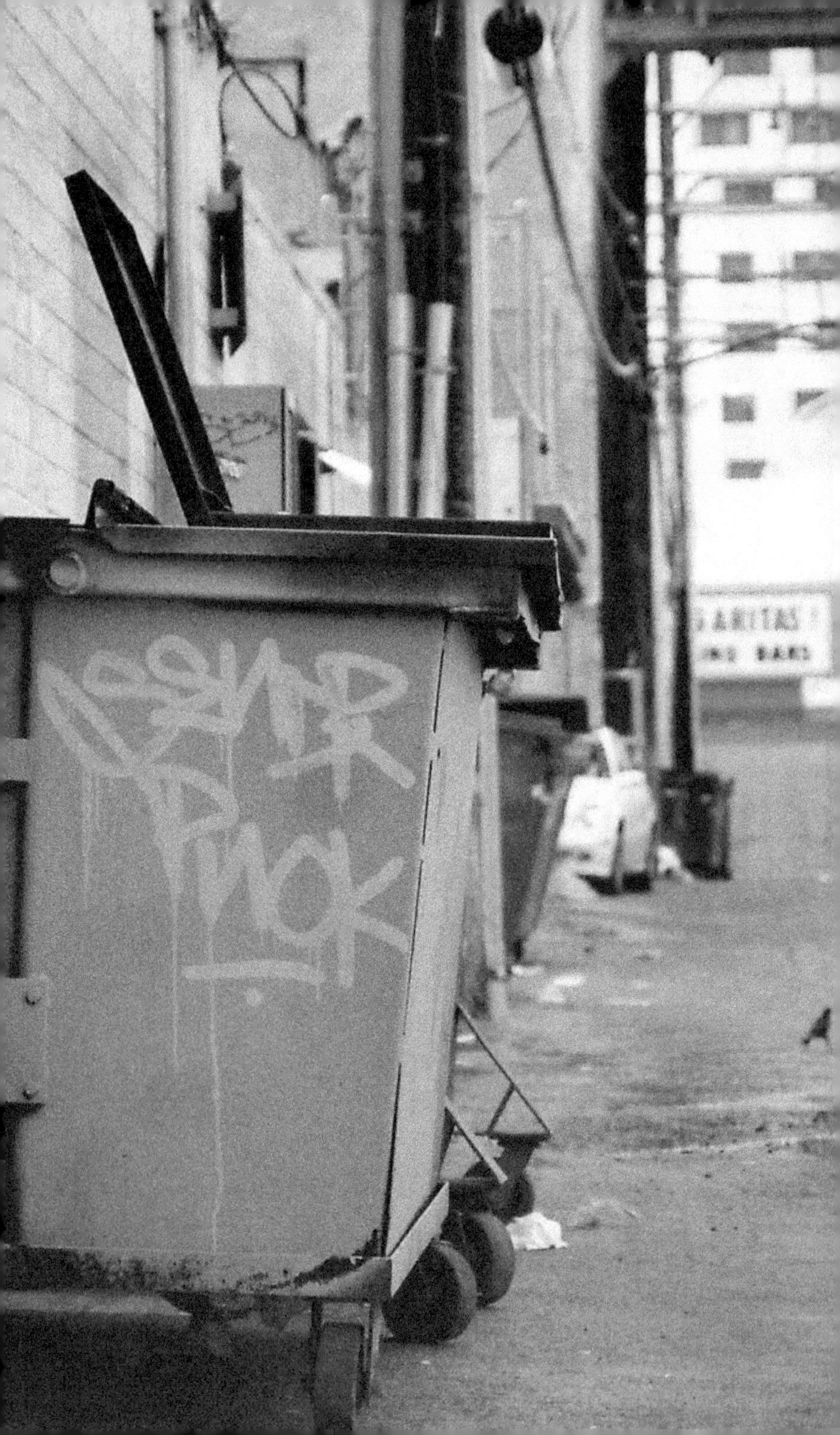

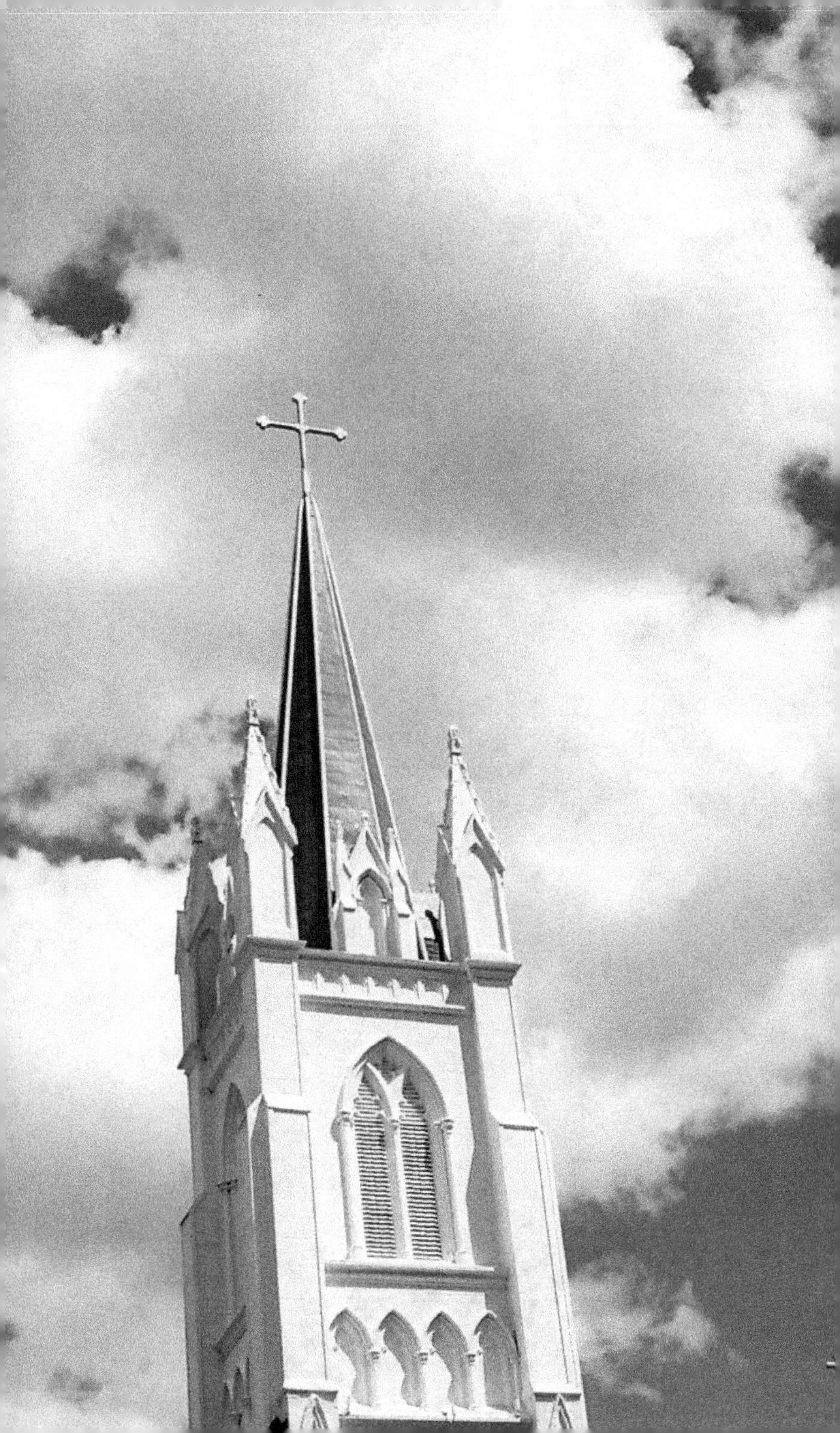

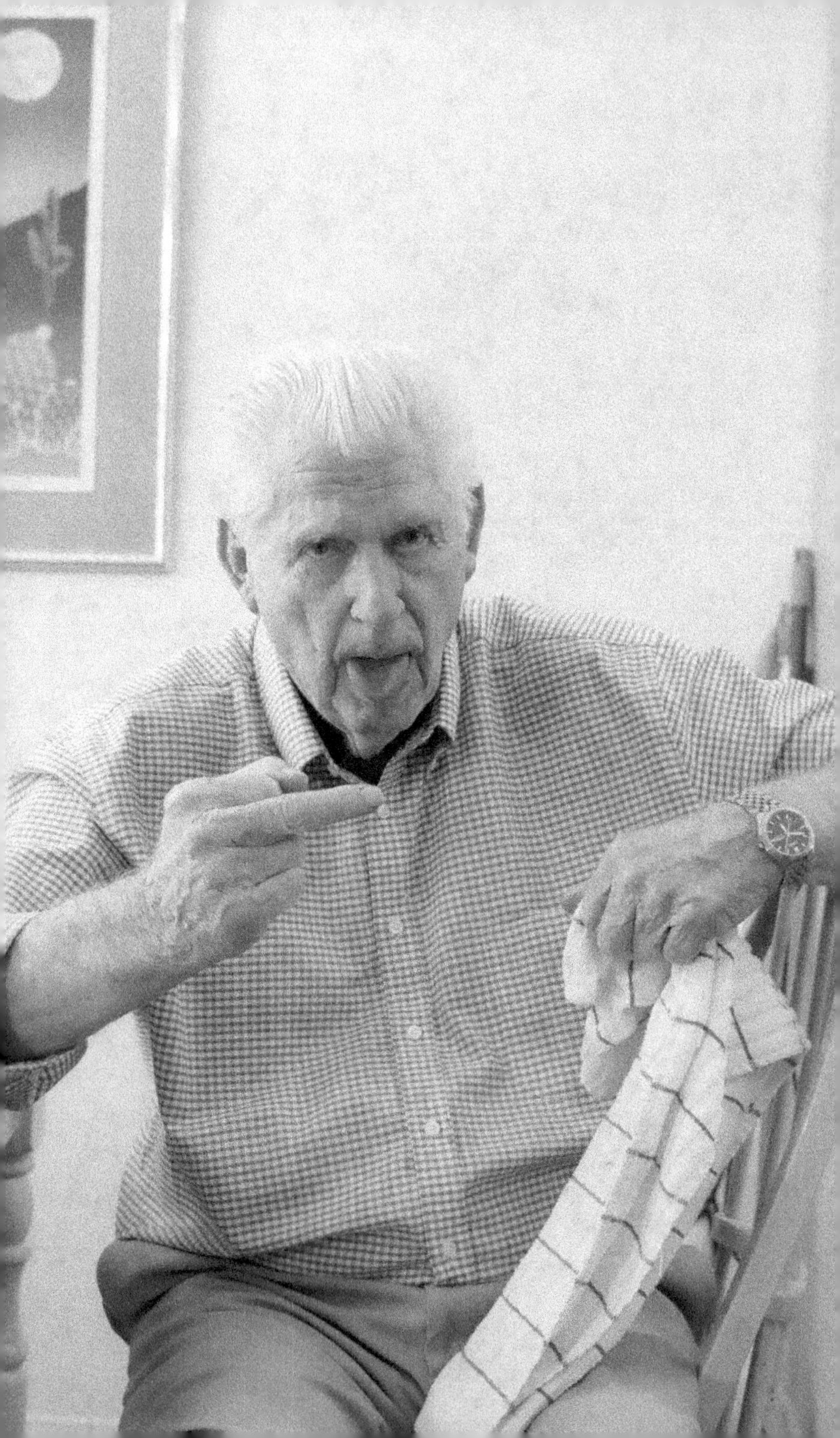

www.ingramcontent.com/pod-product-compliance
Lightning Source LLC
Chambersburg PA
CBHW072039190526
45165CB00018B/1176
* 9 7 8 1 3 8 8 2 9 4 1 6 8 *